DEDICATION

This book is dedicated to the people of Syria who have had their home brutally taken from them. Many of the majestic, beautiful places detailed in this book no longer exist. It is a most painful situation to never be able to return to the place your heart calls home. This book aims to highlight the ingrained magic and mystery of Syria before the war, and the strength and majesty that lives on in its people.

PUBLICATION DETAILS

First edition printed in 2020 in the UK.
ISBN: 978-1-910863-63-3

Author: Malak Al Betare, Nisreen Kanbour and Others.
Editor: Rebecca Joy Novell
Design and Illustration: Alice Charlotte, www.byalicecharlotte.co.uk
Food Photography: Laura Turner, Laurence Hudghton Photography Limited
Prop and Set Styling: Jan Brewer, Laurence Hudghton Photography Limited
Food Stylist: Sally Broom
Portrait and Documentary Photography: Libby Burke Wilde
Contributors: Listed on page 188

Published by Meze Publishing Limited
Unit 1b, 2 Kelham Square
Kelham Riverside
Sheffield S3 8SD
Web: www.mezepublishing.co.uk
Telephone: 0114 275 7709
Email: info@mezepublishing.co.uk

Printed in Great Britain by Bell and Bain Ltd, Glasgow

ACKNOWLEDGEMENTS

Written by Malak Al Betare and Balqis Faroukh.

We would like to show our appreciation to the team of people who helped us showcase a small part of our Syrian culture.

We would first like to thank the beautiful Alice Charlotte, with whom the artistic vision for this project really began. Your kindness towards us made us feel comfortable sharing our dream with you and your hard work has helped us to show our Syrian home in such a positive light.

To Jan, Laura and Sally from Laurence Hudghton Photography, whose endless patience and genuine interest in our recipes made us feel supported and respected. We were always excited to come to the studio, knowing how fun it was working with your team. You made us feel confident and gave us the time and space to express our feelings, speak about our culture, and even speak about ourselves. The beautiful quality of the photographs was an added bonus and we can confidently say you are the most amazing photography team we have ever met.

Thanks also to Libby Burke-Wilde for creating photographs of us and our families which focus on our strength and power, rather than our trauma. You made a special effort to get to know us as people – as mothers, wives, and individuals - and it shines through in the images.

Another thank you is owed to the Lancashire County Council Refugee Integration Team for funding this project, and to Rebecca Joy Novell for providing the support and resources to make our dream possible. A special mention must be made to Salma and Samah who translated many of our meetings and to Rob Herissone-Kelly who formatted all of the recipes.

We are forever grateful for this team of wonderful people and cannot wait for others to try the recipes we have produced in this book, and to learn about our home.

Contents

Syria is made up of 14 governorates, which in Britain, we may refer to as counties. In this book, we have shared recipes from six of the governorates; this is because the vast majority of refugees who have settled in Lancashire have come from these areas. Recipes have also been contributed by Kurdish Syrians and can be found throughout the book.

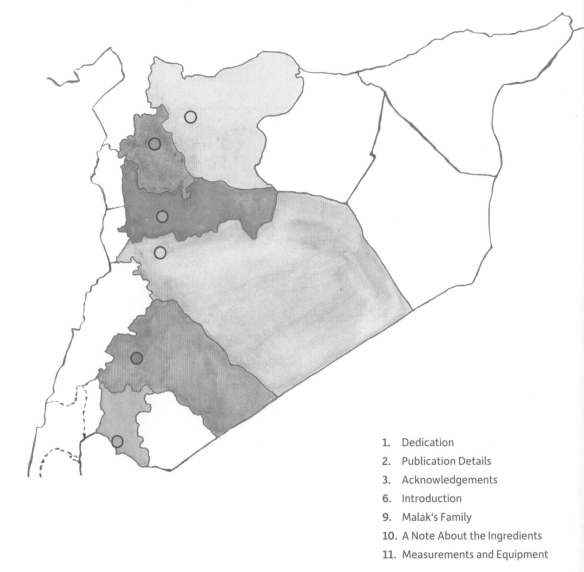

1. Dedication
2. Publication Details
3. Acknowledgements
6. Introduction
9. Malak's Family
10. A Note About the Ingredients
11. Measurements and Equipment

Aleppo (p12-p45)

14. Mariam's Family
15. Nahla's Family
17. Sambusak
19. Ejjeh
20. Falafel
23. Freekeh
25. Mujadara
27. Maejuqat Halbia
29. Molokhia with Rice
31. Kibbeh
32. Fatet Roz
35. Warbat
37. Rice Pudding
39. Baklawa
40. Mushabbak
42. Amina's Family
43. Nisreen's Family

Idlib (p46-p67)

48. Bdour's Family
49. Busaina's Family
51. Kofte
53. Cheese Sambusak
53. Spinach Sambusak
54. Shorbat Al Kodar
57. Batinjan Ma Lahma
59. Shish Barak
60. Mahashe
63. Layali Lubnan
65. Mabrosha

Hama (p68-p89)

70. Walaa's Family
73. Hummus
75. Fatoush
76. Pumpkin Jam
79. Shorbat Addas
81. Mutabbal Batinjan
82. Djej Meshwi
82. Rice and Peas
85. Knafeh
87. Halawat Al Jibn

Homs (p90-p127)

92. Rima's Family
93. Marwa's Family
95. Makdous
97. Muhammara
98. Tabbouleh
101. Muttabal
103. Sfeha
104. Yabrak
107. Ylanji
109. Mandi
110. Kibbeh Hileh
113. Kapsa
115. Okra with Rice
116. Sheikh Al Mahshi
119. Shakriya
121. Basbousa
122. Qatayef Asafiri
125. Kleicha

Damascus (p128-p153)

130. Nareen's Family
131. Kurdish Community
133. Khaliat Nahal
135. Patatas
136. Ful Mudammas
139. Shwarma
141. Harak Osboa
142. Kebab Hindi
145. Beef Kharshouf
145. Vegetarian Kharshouf
147. Balouza
148. Muhallabia
151. Eash Albolbol

Daraa (p154-p187)

156. Balquis' Family
157. Wahiba's Family
159. Juz Muz
161. Fatayer
162. Fattet Hummus
165. Fasulye Wah Bandora
167. Maklouba
168. Kebab Batinjan
171. Mlehy
173. Fried Fish
174. Ghraiba
177. Ma'amoul
179. Barazek
180. Lazakyat
182. Mona's Family
183. About Edah
184. About Asmaa

188. List of Contributors
189. Index

INTRODUCTION

In the UK, when people talk about Syria, the majority think only of the war and destruction that they have seen on the news in recent years and the seven million refugees it has produced. What many people know less about is the beautiful country millions of us called home before it was ravaged by war.

This book began as a small idea in early 2019, when a group of us, as resettled Syrian refugee women in Lancashire, began cooking lunches for our local communities. The lunches were a simple and effective way for us to meet and interact with our English neighbours. Without fail, at every lunch, the food dazzled those trying it for the first time.

After the fifth lunch, and 55th request from diners for some Syrian recipes, we decided that we would put all of our favourite recipes together in one place as a gift for our new friends and neighbours. As the idea grew, we realised what an amazing opportunity this could be to not only educate people about our food, but to also teach people a little about our culture, geography and history.

In the Arab world there is an undeniable relationship between good food and strong families. In this book, we show you the women and the families behind the recipes and show you what Syrian food means to us.

As resettled refugees, we are eternally grateful to England, and particularly Lancashire, for offering us sanctuary and a chance to rebuild our lives. However, Syria will always be our home; our heart. The reality for millions of Syrians is that we will never have the opportunity to return to our childhood homes, our favourite restaurants, the parks we played in, and the offices we worked in. This is not because it is unsafe to do so, but because so many of these places no longer exist. Rebuilding your life from scratch in a foreign country, with a new language and a new culture is a disorientating and often very upsetting process.

INTRODUCTION

During the making of this book, we had the opportunity to share our memories of home and also to think about what parts of home we want to bring with us in our new life. For many, our religion and customs are most important. For others, ensuring our children learn Arabic, as well as English, is critical. With this book, we hope to show you a small glimpse of the things that matter to us and we hope that it promotes a little more understanding of who we are. In our short time here, we have learned that Syrian people and Lancashire folk have a lot in common; we all just want a safe and happy life for ourselves and our children, we want to live in communities that cherish and respect us, we want to be useful and to give back, and of course, we all want to enjoy a delicious home-cooked meal at the end of the day.

Syrian food is slow food.

It is family food.

It is community food.

We hope that when you make the recipes in this book, you take the time to enjoy the process. Many of the recipes can be made with friends or family and will give you the perfect opportunity to spend some quality time together. And of course, we hope that when you serve this food, you serve it to guests, and you serve it with love.

> ## "Malak's patience, dedication, and love for her country has made this book what it is.

Malak Al Betare, Ahmed Al Abboud and their children Mohammed Noor, Dana & Meral

Written by Rebecca Joy Novell

I am sure that Malak will blush reading this, as she is a very modest woman, but it is important to stress what an integral part her family has played in the creation of this book. I have lost count of the mornings she and her husband, Ahmed, invited me round to their house to feed me breakfast, lunch and dinner while we all worked on writing, translating and perfecting the book.

Malak's patience, dedication, and love for her country has made this book what it is. Late nights, hundreds of phone calls and hours of translation are just some elements of the work Malak has undertaken over the last year. She has been an invaluable asset to this book, and I have no doubt that she will be an incredible asset to Lancashire, much like her husband, who within three short years has learned a new language and gained a place studying Mathematics at a prestigious university. Together, they are raising three impressive young children: Noor, who is a kind, calm and clever young man exceeding at his studies; Dana, who is a funny, confident and curious girl; and four year old Meral, who, thanks to her parents' bravery, is starting a safe and happy life in England.

WHERE TO BUY:

Some of the ingredients you will find in these recipes are not available in the large, high street supermarkets. However, smaller Asian continental supermarkets will supply everything you need.

Lemon Salt:
this can be bought in Asian continental stores under this name, or it is otherwise referred to as citric acid.

Ghee:
it is preferable if you buy a tin of ghee but butter can be used as an alternative if necessary.

Pepper Paste:
jars of pepper paste called Biber Salcasi are available in Asian continental stores. It is a Turkish pepper paste. There are hot and mild varieties. Use mild unless otherwise specified.

Pomegranate Molasses:
this is an essential ingredient in Middle Eastern cooking. You can buy it in most larger mainstream superstores.

Mixed Spice:
another essential for Syrian cooking. It can bought ready mixed as it is an aromatic blend of black pepper, coriander, cardamom, nutmeg, ground allspice and cloves.

Vine Leaves:
the vine leaves we use in the Yabrak and Ylanji recipes are the ones packaged in a jar filled with brine.

MEASUREMENTS

Syrian women commonly measure ingredients in cups. We fully recommend that you try the recipes the way they are outlined here, but just in case you need a little help, we have included a conversion table. If you don't have a set of measuring cups then you can use the approximate gram conversions shown here. When using measuring cups, it's important to use the same ones throughout a recipe, and remember that different ingredients weigh different amounts so measurements in grams can't usually be used interchangeably. This table covers the most commonly used ingredients throughout the recipes in this book.

Please note that because there is no single formula for converting cups into other measurements, these are all approximations based on standard US cup measurements (equal to 284ml of water).

CONVERSION TABLE

Ingredient	1 cup	3/4 cup	2/3 cup	1/2 cup	1/3 cup	1/4 cup
Plain or Self-Raising Flour	140g	105g	93g	70g	47g	35g
Cornflour	120g	90g	80g	60g	40g	30g
Caster Sugar	200g	150g	133g	100g	67g	50g
Brown Sugar	170g	128g	113g	85g	57g	43g
Butter, Ghee	225g	169g	150g	113g	75g	56g
Whole Nuts (shelled)	115g	86g	77g	58g	38g	29g
Rice, Lentils, Semolina	200g	150g	113g	100g	67g	50g
Bulgar Wheat	225g	170g	150g	115g	75g	55g
Liquids (Milk, Fruit Juice, Vinegar)	225ml	169ml	150ml	113ml	75ml	56ml
Vegetable Oils	218g	164g	130g	110g	65g	55g
Yoghurt, Tahini	250g	190g	165g	125g	85g	65g
Pomegranate Molasses, Syrup	350g	263g	233g	175g	117g	88g
Peas, Sweetcorn, Pomegranate Seeds	150g	113g	100g	75g	50g	38g
Fresh Herbs	25g	20g	15g	15g	10g	5g
Sultanas	175g	131g	117g	88g	58g	44g
Shredded Coconut, Vermicelli	100g	75g	67g	50g	33g	25g
Sesame Seeds	144g	108g	96g	72g	48g	36g

Aleppo

Written by Shirin Bero

When I think of the landmarks in Aleppo, the ones that come to mind first are The Citadel of Aleppo and the Umayyad Mosque. These are our most important buildings. Al Talil market is also a central part of my city, where you can buy spices, nuts, rugs and much more.

People from Aleppo place great importance on having strong families. Friday is an important day for family bonding. At noon, the men of the house will go to perform the Friday prayer at their local mosque, while the women remain at home and prepare breakfast. After the men return, the whole family will go together to a famous place called Al Muhalaq (Al Sanam). It is an open road for everyone to go to with their relatives and have a community picnic or barbecue while the children can play football in the park. There are sweet sellers dotted around the park selling candy floss, Belila and corn. At night, people spend time at their grandparents' house, where they make desserts and play cards or board games. Friday is, without a doubt, the best day of the week.

Many of my favourite memories from Aleppo are of Eid celebrations. The day before Eid, people go shopping with their children to buy new clothes because it is important to wear new clothes for this celebration. Women will often spend this day making many rich desserts such as ma'amoul and karabeej, which will be given to guests.

Aleppo

On the first day of Eid, men go to perform the Eid prayer and to visit the graves of their dead relatives. There is a distinguished custom, which I personally loved about Eid, where uncles will give children a small gift of money. This gift makes the children very happy and they run around telling their friends and siblings how much money they have collected from the guests, and then they use the money to buy toys.

Eid was very special and beautiful for us when we were children. We used to put the new Eid clothes next to the bed before sleeping and stay up all night in excitement for the first day of Eid, which also meant a day off school. That made us happy. We used to think about the parks we would be allowed to play in and the family members we would meet. I wish I could return to those days.

Syrian food is one of the only things we have left of home

Mariam Nahar, Abedallah Mekhlif and their children Mohammed, Nawar, Hasan and Fatima

Written by Rebecca Joy Novell

Mariam and her husband Abedallah were farmers in southern Aleppo, in Al-Fardoos. Abedallah would also work as a builder when the farming season was quiet. When Mariam began having children, she stayed at home to raise them. Nawar, the youngest son, was only one year old when Mariam and her husband had to leave Syria for Lebanon. Despite this, Nawar still proudly identifies as Syrian. The whole family are proud of their home country. Abedellah told me very confidently that Syrian food is the best in the world and having tasted Mariam's food, I can understand completely why he believes that. "On a serious note," he says, "Syrian food is one of the only things we have left of home. It is very comforting to have a little taste of Syria every day."

The war took everything beautiful from me

Nahla Anbar, Hussain Al Mohammad and their children Rayan, Bayan and Ahmad

Written by Rebecca Joy Novell

Like many Syrian people resettled in other countries, remembering home is very painful for Nahla. "Everything remains in my memory: my home, my family, and my friendly neighbours," she tells me. "My husband was working as a car driver. The war took everything beautiful from me. My mother died a year and a half ago. Although I have lost her, she is in my thoughts every day." The grief of leaving Syria is clear from Nahla's face but she explains that she has to "remain strong" for her children and husband. Resettlement is not an immediate happy ending for refugees. The grief is ongoing, and for many, starting a new life in a new culture with a new language seems an insurmountable task.

Sambusak

[S a m - b u - s a c k]

Sambusak is a traditional stuffed pastry, often referred to as a samosa. In some parts of the Middle East, it is stuffed with braised camel, rather than lamb or beef.

Created by Aysha Jafar

serves 5 | 1h 45 minutes total time | 1h 15 minutes prep time | 30 minutes cooking time

METHOD

1. Place the flour, cumin and half a teaspoon of the salt in a bowl. Stir to distribute everything evenly, then add the water. Stir the mixture well until it forms a dough. Leave the dough in a bowl and cover the bowl with a towel. Leave the covered dough in a warm place for 1 hour.

2. Heat one tablespoon of the vegetable oil in a pan over a medium heat. Add the meat and stir until browned. Add the onion, black pepper and remaining salt. Stir until the onion softens.

3. Take the pan off the heat. Stir in the chopped parsley and leave the mixture to cool.

4. After the dough has been left covered for an hour, remove it from the bowl and cut it into small balls. Use a rolling pin to flatten the balls into thin circles.

5. Put a tablespoon of the meat filling in the centre of each circle. Fold the dough over the mixture to make a semicircle, pressing the edges down firmly to close the sambusak.

6. Heat three tablespoons of vegetable oil in a pan over a medium heat. Fry the sambusak until they become golden.

INGREDIENTS

2 cups plain flour
1/4 tsp cumin
3/4 tsp salt
3/4 cup water
4 tbsp vegetable oil
200g minced beef or lamb
1 onion, diced
1/4 tsp black pepper
1 cup parsley, chopped

Ejjeh

[Eh-ja]

Ejjeh are a type of onion fritter commonly eaten for breakfast in Syria. When courgette is added, the dish is widely known as a Lebanese omelette and can be enjoyed as a light lunch.

Created by Nisreen Kanbour

---

vegetarian

serves 5

50 minutes
total time

30 minutes
prep time

20 minutes
cooking time

METHOD

1. Put the eggs, parsley, garlic, salt and pepper together in a deep bowl and mix the ingredients together. Add the onion and a little olive oil. Stir quickly until the mixture becomes gooey.

2. Add the flour gradually and continue stirring until the mixture has a soft texture.

3. Add some olive oil to a pan and heat at a high temperature for 7 minutes. Before adding the mixture, reduce the heat slightly.

4. Use a tablespoon to separate the mixture out into small circular pieces before placing them carefully into the hot oil.

5. Cook each piece for 1 minute until the bottom turns brown. Then turn and cook until the other side is brown.

6. Once browned, remove the pieces from the oil with a tablespoon and place them on kitchen paper to soak up any excess oil.

7. Serve the ejjeh with yoghurt and salad.

INGREDIENTS

6 eggs
1 cup parsley, chopped
1 clove of garlic, crushed
$\frac{1}{2}$ tsp salt
8 tsp black pepper
1 onion, finely chopped
$\frac{1}{2}$ cup olive oil
6 tbsp plain flour

Falafel

Falafel has been enjoyed in the Middle East for thousands of years and has now become a popular street food around the world. Mariam's Aleppo-style falafel is perfect for on-the-go lunches or for feeding hungry children.

Created by Mariam Nahar

| vegan | serves 5 | 24h 30 minutes total time | 24 hours soaking time | 15 minutes prep time | 10-15 minutes cooking time |

METHOD

1. Place the soaked chickpeas into a blender. Add the chopped onions and parsley and mix at medium speed until the mixture becomes a smooth dough.

2. Transfer the mixture into a deep bowl. Add the salt, ground coriander, chopped garlic, cumin and baking soda then stir until well combined.

3. Divide the mixture into small, even portions and press into round pieces with your palms. Push your finger through the middle of each piece to create a doughnut shape.

4. Heat the oil in a wide pan over a medium heat until the oil is simmering. Carefully place the falafel pieces directly into the hot oil, turning until browned all over.

5. Carefully remove the falafel pieces from the oil, drain off any excess and serve hot.

INGREDIENTS

500g chickpeas, soaked in water for 24 hours prior to cooking
1 medium onion, finely chopped
1 tbsp parsley, finely chopped
1 tbsp salt
1 tbsp ground coriander
4 cloves of garlic, peeled and finely chopped
1 tbsp cumin
1 tbsp baking soda
1 litre vegetable oil, for frying

For a more professional finish, you can use a falafel scoop which is available online.

Freekeh

[Free-car]

Freekeh is an ancient cereal made from durum wheat, which remains a staple ingredient across much of the Mediterranean and Middle East. This hearty dish combines freekeh with a flavoursome broth that can be made with either lamb or chicken.

Created by Jihan Bero

 serves 5

 1h 55 minutes total time

 10 minutes prep time

 1h 45 minutes cooking time

METHOD

1. Place the meat in a large pot and pour the water over the meat so that it is completely submerged. Put the pot over a high heat until the water comes to the boil, then reduce to a medium heat. Add the salt, black pepper, onion, ginger, cardamom, cinnamon, bay leaves and dried lemon then leave the broth to cook for 1 hour and 10 minutes.

2. In another cooking pot, melt three tablespoons of the ghee over a medium heat then add the freekeh. Cook the freekeh for 5 minutes, stirring the mixture continuously.

3. Carefully ladle 12 cups of the meat broth over the freekeh (leaving the meat behind), stirring it well and ensuring the freekeh is fully submerged. Bring the mixture to the boil then reduce the heat. Leave the mixture to simmer over a low heat for 30 minutes or until the freekeh is soft.

4. In a separate pan, melt the remaining tablespoon of ghee over a medium heat. Add the peas and leave to cook until they are soft, stirring occasionally. When the peas are cooked, put them to one side. Once the freekeh is ready, layer the meat on top and serve with a decoration of peas and roasted cashew nuts.

INGREDIENTS

1kg lamb or chicken, diced
3 litres water
1 tsp salt
1 tsp black pepper
1 medium onion, diced
$\frac{1}{2}$ tsp ground ginger
8 cardamom pods
2 cinnamon sticks
3 bay leaves
1 dried lemon
4 tbsp ghee
4 cups freekeh
3 cups frozen peas
handful of cashews, roasted

Mujadara

[Moo-jah-da-ra]

Mujadara (or Mujadarra) is one of the rare vegan dishes you will find in Syrian cuisine. Despite the simple ingredients, this dish is full of flavour and has been adopted as a staple dish by many Syrian families.

Created by Mariam Nahar

vegan | serves 5 | 1h 15 minutes total time | 15 minutes prep time | 1 hour cooking time

METHOD

1. Wash and drain the lentils thoroughly before placing them in a pan. Cover them with the water and leave on a medium heat. Once the water has come to the boil, cover the pan with a lid and leave the lentils to simmer on a low heat. After 20 minutes, take the lentils off the heat and leave to one side.

2. Wash the bulgur wheat before adding it to a clean pan along with the olive oil. Over a medium heat, fry the bulgur wheat in oil for 10 minutes. Stir the mixture frequently while cooking.

3. Add the lentils, including the water they were boiled in, as well as the stock cubes, salt, cumin and black pepper. Stir well. Cover the pan with a lid and leave the mixture to boil for 10 minutes, then reduce the heat to low and leave the mixture to simmer for a further 10 minutes.

4. Meanwhile, place another pan over a medium heat and add a splash of olive oil. Once the oil is hot, add the sliced onions. Stirring regularly, cook the onions until golden brown.

5. Pour the mujadara into a bowl and serve with the fried onions on top.

INGREDIENTS

½ cup brown lentils
1.5 litres water
3 cups coarse bulgur wheat
¾ cup olive oil
2 vegetable stock cubes
1 tsp salt
1 tsp cumin
1 tsp black pepper
2 large onions, sliced

Maejuqat Halbia

[Maa-joo-ka Hal-be-ah]

Maejuqat Halbia is one of the less well known dishes from Syria. They appear to be simple lamb burgers but are actually stuffed with a mix of cheese and vegetables.

Created by Sherin Bero

serves 8   2h 30 minutes total time   2h minutes prep time   30 minutes cooking time

METHOD

1. Put the minced lamb into a bowl and add a pinch of the salt, a pinch of black pepper and mixed spice. Mix the ingredients well, ensuring the meat is evenly coated. Use your palms to shape the lamb into 8 evenly sized balls. Wet the meatballs with cold water and place them on a baking tray. Leave the tray in the fridge for 30 minutes.

2. Place a pan over a medium heat and add a tablespoon of ghee. Once the ghee has melted, add the chopped onions and stir for 3 minutes. Add the sliced mushrooms and stir for a further 5 minutes, then add the diced peppers and sweetcorn along with a pinch of salt and black pepper and let the mixture cook for another 10 minutes, stirring regularly. Once the vegetables have softened, take the pan off the heat and leave the mixture to cool.

3. Spread the other tablespoon of ghee over a baking tray and preheat the oven to 120°C. Place a piece of greaseproof paper on a small side plate. Put one of the meatballs on top. Wet your hands and press the meatball into a thin circle, using the plate as a template for size.

4. Spread 3 tablespoons of the vegetable mixture on top of the meat patty, then top with grated cheese. Place a piece of greaseproof paper on another plate of the same size, and form a second meat patty. Place this on top of the vegetables and cheese then press the edges down, sealing the filling inside. Remove the greaseproof paper and carefully place the maejuqat on the greased baking tray. Repeat this process until all the lamb, vegetable mixture and cheese have been used up.

5. Place the tray on the middle shelf of the preheated oven and leave the maejuqat to cook for about 30 minutes, or until the meat is well browned. Remove them from the oven and leave to cool before serving.

INGREDIENTS

1kg minced lamb
$1/2$ tsp of salt
$1/2$ tsp ground black pepper
pinch of mixed spice, to taste
2 tbsp ghee
2 medium onions, chopped
200g mushrooms, sliced
200g red pepper, diced
$1/2$ cup sweetcorn
300g mozzarella, grated

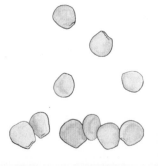

We suggest serving the maejuqat halbia alongside rice and vermicelli, with garlic mayo or tahini sauce.

Molokhia with Rice

[M o l - o h - k e e - y a]

Molokhia (or mulukhiya) is the name of both a plant and a dish. Also referred to as jute or Jew's mallow, molokhia leaves are rich in nutrients such as iron and vitamin C and are classed as a 'superfood'.

Created by Nisreen Kanbour

serves 5 | 2h 10 minutes total time | 35 minutes soaking time | 10 minutes prep time | 1h 25 minutes cooking time

METHOD

1. Remove the stems from the dried jute and soak the leaves in a bowl of warm water. After 35 minutes, remove the leaves from the bowl and firmly press the water out of them, squeezing them into balls with your hands, before setting them to one side.

2. Place the chicken breast into a pan of water and bring to the boil. Once boiled, add the salt and pepper, then reduce to a medium heat and leave to cook for 30 minutes. Remove the chicken from the water, keeping the broth for later, and shred into small pieces.

3. Place a cooking pot over a medium heat and add the sunflower oil. Once the oil is hot, add the garlic and shredded chicken breast and cook until the meat has browned, stirring regularly. Add the jute leaves to the mixture and stir together well. Add 1 litre of the chicken broth and the chicken stock cubes to the pot and bring the mixture to the boil. Leave to cook on a low heat for 15 minutes.

4. Add the ghee to a separate pan and fry the vermicelli until it has turned golden brown. Add the rice and fry for a further 2 minutes. Add two cups of boiling water, bring to the boil and leave for 3 minutes. Reduce the heat to the lowest setting and leave to simmer with a lid on for 35 minutes.

5. Serve the molokhia and vermicelli rice together.

INGREDIENTS

150g dried jute (molokhia) leaves
440g chicken breast
1 tsp salt
1 tsp ground black pepper
5 tbsp sunflower oil
3 tbsp garlic, crushed
1.5 litres water
2 chicken stock cubes
1 tbsp ghee
$1/2$ cup dried vermicelli
1 cup basmati rice

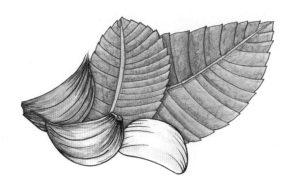

Kibbeh

[Kuh-bah]

Kibbeh is arguably the best-loved and most famous dish in Syria. It comes in a myriad of forms including baked, fried and grilled. Each region in Syria claims to have the best kibbeh but we are pretty confident you'll be happy with Amina's fried kibbeh from Aleppo.

Created by Amina Al Hassan

serves 6-8   1h 15 minutes total time   45 minutes prep time   30 minutes cooking time

METHOD (for the filling)

1. Place a pan over a medium heat and add the oil. When hot, add the diced onions and stir for 5 minutes until they are golden brown. Add the meat along with the black pepper, seven spice mix and cayenne pepper then stir for another 10 minutes until the meat has browned. Stir in the ground pine nuts then take the mixture off the heat.

METHOD (for the bulgur dough)

2. Prepare the bulgur wheat by leaving it to soak in the hot water for 30 minutes until it softens. Grind the softened bulgur in a blender along with the salt, cumin, coriander and cayenne pepper until the ingredients form a smooth dough, then separate this dough into balls approximately 4cm across.

3. To form the kibbeh, create a hole in the middle of the ball of dough, then press the inside to create a thin wall. Place two teaspoons of the meat filling in the centre of each piece. Close the dough around the meat to seal the filling inside.

4. Half-fill a pan with vegetable oil and place it over a medium heat. When the oil is hot, add the kibbeh. You might want to do this in batches depending on the size of your pan. Leave them to fry until golden brown, turning each one occasionally, then remove the kibbeh and place them on a paper towel to absorb the excess oil.

INGREDIENTS

for the filling:
3 tbsp vegetable oil
3 medium onions, diced
500g minced lamb
$\frac{1}{2}$ tbsp ground black pepper
$\frac{1}{2}$ tbsp seven spice mix
1 tbsp cayenne pepper
50g pine nuts, ground

for the bulgur dough:
1kg fine bulgur wheat
1 litre hot water
1 tbsp salt
$\frac{1}{2}$ tsp ground cumin
$\frac{1}{2}$ tsp ground coriander
1 tbsp cayenne pepper
vegetable oil, for deep frying

We recommend serving hot with Arabic bread, plain yoghurt for dipping and a cucumber salad.

Fatet Roz

[Fat-et Ruz]

Nareen's family are Kurdish and originate from Kobani. This dish is a favourite with her husband and three young daughters. The combination of rice and chicken makes it a great choice for even the fussiest of young eaters!

Created by Nareen Orfali

serves 6 | 1h 45 minutes total time | 15 minutes prep time | 1h 30 minutes cooking time

METHOD (for the fatet roz)

1. Put the chicken into a cooking pot then add enough water to completely submerge the meat. Place it over a medium heat and bring the water to the boil, then add the salt, black pepper, cinnamon, cardamom, bay leaves, dried lemon and mixed spice. Leave the broth to cook on a medium heat for 45 minutes.

2. Soak the rice in warm water for 30 minutes with a teaspoon of salt. In another pot, heat some oil over a medium heat. Drain the soaked rice and add it to the pot with the oil. Stir well for 2 minutes, then pour 4 cups of the chicken broth over the rice, leaving the spices and chicken behind, and leave the mixture to come to the boil. When it is boiling, reduce the heat and leave it to simmer on a low heat for 30 minutes with the lid on, stirring occasionally.

3. Cut the Arabic bread into medium-sized squares. Add the oil to a frying pan over a medium heat, then fry the pieces of bread until golden. Leave them to one side to cool.

4. Carefully remove the chicken from the bone, then take the pan used for frying the bread, add a little more oil and fry the pieces of chicken over a medium heat with a little salt and pepper until cooked.

5. Combine the yoghurt, tahini and crushed garlic in a bowl. Stir well, add the lemon juice and about two ladlesful of the broth then stir continuously until the ingredients are well combined.

TO SERVE

6. Use a deep dish. Spread half a cup of the yoghurt sauce across the bottom of the dish, then top that with a layer of the fried bread pieces. Then add a layer of broth, followed by another layer of yoghurt sauce. Top this layer with chicken and rice and decorate with roasted cashews and the remaining fried bread.

INGREDIENTS

for the fatet roz:
1kg chicken (legs and thighs)
generous pinch of salt
1 tsp black pepper
2 cinnamon sticks
5 cardamom pods
2 bay leaves
1 dried lemon
1 tsp mixed spice
500g basmati rice
1 litre vegetable oil
2 loaves Arabic bread of your choice
4 cups plain yoghurt
1 cup tahini
1 tbsp garlic, crushed
¼ cup lemon juice

to serve:
handful of cashews, roasted

Warbat

You may be forgiven for thinking that warbat is another type of baklawa. The sweet and flaky pastry makes them very similar. Warbat can be made with a variety of fillings from custard to pistachios or sweet cheese. This treat will satisfy any sweet tooth.

Created by Amina Al Hassan

| vegetarian | serves 12 | 50 minutes total time | 20 minutes prep time | 30 minutes cooking time |

METHOD (for the warbat)

1. To prepare the cream, pour the milk into a pan and put it over a medium heat. Stir constantly to avoid the milk sticking to the bottom of the pan. When it starts to come to the boil, add the vinegar and stir well for about 3 minutes. When the milk starts to separate into lumps of curd and yellow liquid, take it off the heat. Remove the milk curds with a sieve and leave them to one side to dry.

2. When the milk curds have dried and solidified, place them in a bowl and add the mascarpone. Mix well until the curds and the mascarpone are well combined.

3. To prepare the warbat, roll out the filo pastry into a sheet, making sure the thickness is even. Cut the sheet into 25 equal squares. Fold each square over to form a triangle, only pressing lightly so you can open them again later. At this point, preheat the oven to 170°C.

4. Brush a baking tray with melted ghee then place the triangular pieces of pastry on the tray. Cover the pieces of pastry with the remaining ghee. Put the tray on the middle shelf of the oven and leave the pastry to cook for 15 to 20 minutes, until golden brown.

METHOD (for the syrup)

5. While the pastry is in the oven, you can prepare the sugar syrup. Add the sugar and water to a pan. Stir continually until the sugar has dissolved, place the pan over a high heat and bring to the boil. Add the lemon salt or lemon juice and reduce the heat for 7 minutes. Take it off the heat and leave the syrup to cool.

TO SERVE

6. Remove the pastry triangles from the oven and pour the syrup over them. Leave the pastry to cool then open each piece and fill the warbat with the mascarpone cream. Decorate with ground pistachios before serving.

INGREDIENTS

for the warbat:
2 litres whole milk
½ cup white vinegar
170g mascarpone
470g ready-made filo pastry
200g ghee, melted

for the syrup:
1 cup water
2 cups sugar
¼ tsp lemon salt or
½ tsp lemon juice

to serve:
pistachio nuts, ground, to decorate

Rice Pudding

Variations of rice pudding exist all over the world and can be topped with any number of different ingredients, including cinnamon or raisins. Nahla's rice pudding uses the traditional flavours of rose and pistachio, resulting in a simple and tasty dessert.

Created by Nahla

vegetarian   serves 5   1h 40 minutes total time   1h 15 minutes prep time   25 minutes cooking time

METHOD (for the pudding)

1. Wash the rice thoroughly to remove any excess starch and leave it to soak in a bowl of warm water for 10 minutes. Drain the rice and place it in a pan. Cover the rice with the water and put the pan over a medium heat. Bring the water to the boil and leave the rice to cook for 10 minutes before taking the pan off the heat and leaving it to one side.

2. In a separate pan, combine the milk and cornstarch. Put the mixture over a low heat and stir until the cornstarch dissolves. When they are thoroughly combined, add the cooked rice and the sugar. Put the pan on a low heat and stir the mixture constantly for 15 minutes.

3. Take the pan off the heat and place the rice pudding into a bowl. Leave the mixture to cool in the fridge for 1 hour before serving.

TO SERVE

4. If you like, serve the rice pudding with a decorative garnish of crushed pistachios and rose petals.

INGREDIENTS

for the pudding:
¹/₂ cup short grain rice
250ml water
800ml whole milk
1¹/₂ tbsp cornstarch
¹/₂ cup granulated sugar

to serve (optional):
handful of pistachio nuts, crushed
rose petals

Baklawa

[Bah-klow-ah]

Baklawa has made its way over to Europe in many different forms. Famous in Greece, Turkey and many other Arabic countries, we are confident that Nareen's Kurdish variation will be your new favourite!

Created by Nareen Orfarli

serves 8

45 minutes
total time

30 minutes
prep time

15 minutes
cooking time

METHOD (for the baklawa)

1. Place the 400g of pistachios in a blender with the orange blossom water and blend until fine.

2. Remove two filo pastry sheets from the pack and keep the rest of the pastry covered to prevent it from drying out. Brush the first layer of pastry with melted ghee. Place the second layer of pastry on top of the first and brush the top with ghee.

3. Spread two tablespoons of pistachio mixture along the longest edge of the pastry. Roll the pastry around the mixture like a swiss roll. Repeat this process using two more sheets of pastry each time, brushed with ghee and layered, until all the filling has been used up. Meanwhile, preheat the oven to 180°C.

4. Coat a baking tray with ghee and place each roll on it. Before cooking, cut the baklawa as desired, either in squares or triangles. Pour the remaining ghee over the top so that all of the baklawa is covered.

5. Place the tray on the middle shelf of the preheated oven and bake for 15 minutes. When the baklawa are golden brown, they are ready.

FOR THE SYRUP

6. Pour the water into a clean pan, add the sugar and stir continuously until the sugar has dissolved. Put the pan over a medium heat, when the mixture starts to come to the boil, add the lemon juice. While the baklawa are still hot, pour the sugar syrup over them and decorate with pistachios before serving.

INGREDIENTS

for the baklawa:
400g pistachios, plus extra for decoration
2 tbsp orange blossom water
450g filo dough, thawed
250g ghee, melted

for the sugar syrup:
1 cup sugar
3/4 cup water
1/2 tsp lemon juice

Mushabbak

[Moo-shab-ack]

Mushabbak will remind you of the sweet Spanish snack, churros.
This deep-fried treat is a favourite amongst Syrian children.
Created by Nisreen Kanbour and Mohammad Ajam

vegetarian   serves 8   1h 20 minutes total time   1h 15 minutes prep time   5 minutes cooking time

METHOD (for the mushabbak)

1. In a bowl, mix the semolina, flour, yoghurt, water and baking powder. Stir well until the ingredients are fully combined and form a wet dough. Cover the bowl with cling film and leave the dough to one side. After the dough has been left to rest for 1 hour, transfer it into a piping bag.

2. Pour enough vegetable oil for shallow frying into a wide, deep pan and heat it gently. When the oil is sizzling hot, pipe a small amount of the mixture into the pan, forming a circle of dough. Repeat this with the rest of the mixture, working in batches depending on how large your pan is. Cook the mushabbak until they are golden, moving them around the pan to ensure they don't stick.

METHOD (for the syrup)

3. Mix the sugar and water together until the sugar dissolves. Put the mixture on a low heat and leave it to boil. Once it has boiled, add the lemon juice and leave it to boil for a further 2 minutes. Turn off the heat and leave the syrup to cool.

TO SERVE

4. Put the warm mushabbak on a plate along with a bowl of the syrup for dipping.

INGREDIENTS

for the mushabbak:
½ cup semolina
1 cup self-raising flour
1 cup plain yoghurt
1 cup water
1 tsp baking powder
1 litre vegetable oil

for the syrup:
3 cups sugar
6 cups water
1 tsp lemon juice

You will need a piping bag for this recipe.

Everyone we know has left Syria

Amina Al Hassan, Mohammad Al Ahmad and
their children Riad, Marwa, Ahmad and Emma

Written by Rebecca Joy Novell

Mohammad and Amina lived in the Aleppo countryside. Mohammad grew up with nine brothers and four sisters. "The house was always busy," he told me. His eldest sister was born in 1972 and his youngest brother in 1995, so the house was always full of children. When Mohammad turned 16 he began raising cattle on his father's farm. Mohammad told me: "I always knew I was going to work for my father, there was never any other plan. I miss those childhood memories of all the family working together."

Amina and Mohammad knew each other through family. They married in 2006 and moved out of Mohammad's family home. Mohammad used his skills to work on farms in Lebanon and Amina raised their three boys at home. When the war began, they had to move to the border near Turkey when their youngest son was just a few months old.

When I asked them what they missed most about home, they told me: "We miss our family, of course. We miss nights out with our friends. Because we lived in the countryside, there were no restaurants, so we would eat at home before we went out then meet up at each other's houses and play cards and talk for hours and hours. It was a happy life. Now our friends are spread out all over the world. Everyone we know has left Syria."

Their daughter, Emma, was born in England and is named after the woman who volunteered with a Lancashire charity to help welcome the family and settle them in the UK.

"woodwork is part of the country's heart and soul"

Nisreen Kanbour, Mohammad Ajam and their children Abed, Joudi, Ahmad and Layan

Written by Rebecca Joy Novell

Nisreen and her husband Mohammad are from Aleppo. Before the war, Mohammad worked as a carpenter. Carpentry is a huge trade in Syria; cities such as Saqba are known throughout the Levant as 'The City of Furniture' and woodwork is part of the country's heart and soul. For centuries, the art of intricate woodwork design has been passed on from father to son. Furnishings are not meant to merely be practical; instead they are things of beauty, with each door, cabinet and chair being a unique and ornate creation. The most famous and recognisable style of woodwork from the region is Syrian inlaying, where mother of pearl, metals and other materials are laid in the wood to create a mosaic style. This technique is steeped in Islamic tradition and goes back thousands of years. The Ummayad Mosque is notably covered with this inlaying style. Unfortunately, Mohammad's incredible woodwork skills are not as sought after in England, and so he and Nisreen are hoping to open a Syrian Sweet Shop.

Citadel of Aleppo, 2006

Idlib

written by Ibrahim Shawish

My name is Ibrahim Shawish. I am from Syria. I was born in the city of Jisr al-Shughur, which sits on the Orontes River in the Governorate of Idlib. Jisr al-Shughur is famous for its production of olives, olive oil, apples and citrus fruits. We are also renowned for our strength in growing almonds, sesame seeds and figs.

Jisr al-Shughur is one of many cities in Idlib. Idlib is divided into six districts: Ashrafiyeh, Hurriya, Hittin, Hejaz, Downtown and al-Qusur. Other cities include Kafr Yahmul to the north, Maarrat al-Ikhwan and Zardana in the north east and Binnish and Kafriya to the south. Idlib is often seen as the holiday destination of choice for many Syrians due to its beautiful scenery and temperate climate. Frequent rains not only help our crops to grow but produce lush, green mountainous scenery.

Idlib has seen many different civilizations settle in it, including Roman, Eblan and Byzantine. Because of this, we have nearly 200 ancient monuments embedded in our landscapes, including castles and tombs. Due to Idlib being a long-established

Idlib

region, we are famous for our 'Dead Cities' or 'Forgotten Cities'. These 700 sites are a combination of pagan and Christian churches and monuments that were abandoned around the 8th century. They are now recognized as UNESCO World Heritage Sites.

I have so many fond memories of Idlib. The most important days of my life, such as my student days, took place in Jisr al-Shughur. Life was simple there and the people loved each other very much. In 2012, I was forced to leave because of the war.

Note from Rebecca Joy Novell

It is important to note that at the time of writing (16th February 2020), the civil war in Syria has seen another escalation and Idlib is currently the new front line of the conflict. Over the last nine years of the war, the population of Idlib has increased from 1.5 million to 3 million, due to internal displacement of Syrian citizens. The UN are currently warning of an imminent "humanitarian catastrophe" as one million Syrians are living in dire conditions in refugee camps along the border with Turkey.

I always enjoyed sitting with my mum and cooking together

Bdour Sayoof

Written by Bdour Sayoof

My happiest memories of home are living with my parents and friends, all in the same area of the city of Homs. My mother was the one who taught me to cook. I was 14 years old when I began learning. I always enjoyed sitting with my mum and cooking together. My favourite dish that she cooked was Kibbeh (page 31), which is not an easy dish to make and so my mum would make it when we were expecting guests or celebrating something.

I miss the life we used to enjoy with our friends and neighbours. Every Friday, our family would meet with all our friends at the park or by the river and we would enjoy a communal barbecue together. We would agree on one person to buy all the meat for the barbecue and everyone else would bring a sweet dish or a fruit salad from home. Our social life was so amazing in Syria.

"We love eating together as a family"

Abdol Kader Hijar and Busaina Ismail

Written by Rebecca Joy Novell

Busaina and Abdol are a very pious and respectful couple. They have lived in England for three years and have learned the language with ease. However, they stressed to me the importance of their three children learning Arabic. Like many refugee families, the children have no memories of Syria and so Syrian culture and language is something they only experience within the home.

Abdol and Busaina speak of Syria with such fondness. They tell me: "We want British people to learn about our home. It is a very special place. The weather, particularly during the summer, which is four months long, is wonderful. We have tourist attractions, monuments, wonderful beaches and the sea. Syrian people are very hospitable. Our way of life in Syria is wonderful." Busaina explains to me that "in Syria you can spend the whole day cooking. It is slow food and can be quite tiring but it is a labour of love. You are cooking for your whole family. We love eating together as a family."

Kofte

[Kof-tah]

*Kofte is most famously made with meat but Aysha's Kurdish version is
a fantastic vegan alternative.*
Created by Aysha Sharaf Jaafar

| vegan | serves 8 | 1 hour total time | 55 minutes prep time | 5 minutes cooking time |

METHOD

1. Soak the bulgur wheat in the warm water for about 30 minutes, and once the water has been absorbed add the salt, black pepper, mint and tomato purée.

2. Mix the ingredients together then knead the mixture for about 10 minutes. If the mixture becomes dry, sprinkle a little of the cold water over it. When you get a soft mixture that sticks together well, stop adding water but keep kneading for another 10 minutes to get a supple dough. During this time, add the chopped parsley and mix it in thoroughly.

3. Put a tablespoon of the olive oil into a pan on a medium heat. Once the oil is hot, add the chopped spring onions and stir until they turn golden in colour. Add the spring onions to the bulgur dough along with the remaining olive oil and mix thoroughly for about 5 minutes.

4. Divide the dough into balls and lightly roll each one between your palms to get the distinctive elongated shape of kofte.

INGREDIENTS

3 cups fine bulgur wheat
2 cups warm water
2 tsp salt
1 tsp black pepper
1 tbsp fresh chopped mint
1 tbsp tomato purée
1 cup cold water
1 bunch parsley, finely chopped
1 cup olive oil
4 spring onions, finely chopped

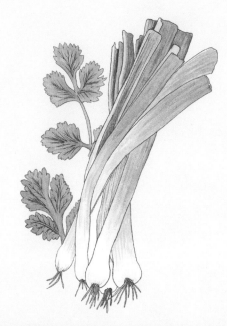

Sambusak

[Sam-bu-sack]

Cheese sambusak have been enjoyed in Syria for thousands of years. They can be eaten as a treat at any time but these buttery pastries filled with gooey cheese are a particular favourite during Ramadan. Batoul has also provided an alternative spinach version below. .

Created by Batoul Einja

Cheese Sambusak

vegetarian

serves 5

35 minutes total time

20 minutes prep time

15 minutes cooking time

METHOD

1. Before you start, preheat the oven to 180°C.

2. Place the mozzarella and halloumi in a bowl with the chopped parsley, nigella seeds, black pepper and salt. Stir well until all of the ingredients are mixed together.

3. On a flat surface, roll the filo pastry into a thin sheet with a rolling pin. Cut the pastry into long rectangle sections. Place one teaspoon of the cheese mixture at the edge of each rectangle of pastry, then wrap the pastry over the filling several times to form a triangle. Repeat this for each piece until all the pastry and filling is used up. Brush a small amount of the egg white onto the edges of the pastry to seal.

4. Lightly coat a baking tray with the oil, making sure it is spread evenly. Place the sambusak on the tray and put it in the preheated oven for 15 minutes. Serve warm.

INGREDIENTS

1kg mozzarella cheese, chopped
450g halloumi cheese, diced
3 tbsp chopped parsley
1 tbsp nigella seeds
1/4 tsp black pepper
1/4 tsp salt
1 packet of filo pastry
1 egg white
1 tbsp vegetable oil

Spinach Sambusak

vegetarian

serves 8

40 minutes total time

10 minutes prep time

40 minutes cooking time

METHOD

1. Before you start, preheat the oven to 180°C. Wash the chopped spinach well and place it in a bowl. Add a pinch of salt and mix it into the spinach, draining off any excess water.

2. Put a pot over a medium heat and add a splash of olive oil. When the oil is hot, add the diced onion and stir well until it turns golden. Add the pepper paste and stir well. Add the chopped spinach along with the sumac, cumin, black pepper and lemon salt. Stir well then leave the mixture to cook on a low heat for 10 minutes, stirring occasionally.

3. Remove the pan from the heat and drain off any excess liquid before leaving the mixture to cool. Roll out the filo pastry and cut the sheet into long rectangle sections. Place a spoonful of the spinach filling onto the edge of each rectangle of pastry, then wrap the pastry over the filling several times to form a triangle. Repeat this for each piece until all the pastry and filling is used up. Brush a small amount of the egg white onto the edges of the pastry to seal.

4. Spread a little olive oil over a baking tray. Place the sambusak on the tray and cook in the preheated oven for about 15 minutes until the pastry is golden. Remove from the oven and serve hot with a drizzle of pomegranate molasses.

INGREDIENTS

3kg spinach, chopped
pinch of salt, to taste
olive oil
1 medium onion, diced
1 tbsp pepper paste
1 tsp sumac
1 tsp ground cumin
1 tsp black pepper
1 tsp lemon salt
1 pack of ready-made filo pastry
1 egg, separated
1/2 tbsp pomegranate molasses

Shorbat Al Kodar

[Shor-bet Al Hood-ar]

Shorbat al kodar is what we would refer to as vegetable soup and like all good vegetable soups, you can use whatever you have left in the fridge at the end of the week. Lentils can also be added to thicken the mixture, if you wish.

Created by Batoul Einja

vegan

serves 5

45 minutes
total time

30 minutes
prep time

15 minutes
cooking time

METHOD

1. Place a cooking pot over a medium heat and add the vegetable oil. When the oil is hot, add the diced onion and a pinch of salt. Stir well for 2 minutes as the onions fry.

2. Add the carrot and potato, stir well then add the rest of the salt, the black pepper, curry powder and vegetable stock powder. Mix the ingredients together well and leave the mixture to cook for 8 minutes, stirring occasionally.

3. Add the green beans and peas and stir for another 2 minutes. Boil the water in a kettle then add it to the mixture. When the water is boiling in the pot, add the vermicelli and the cauliflower. Leave the broth to cook for 20 minutes before taking it off the heat. Serve the shorbat al kodar in bowls and decorate with the chopped parsley.

INGREDIENTS

¹/₄ cup vegetable oil
1 medium onion, diced
1 tbsp salt
1 cup carrots, peeled and chopped
1 cup potatoes, peeled and chopped
1 tsp ground black pepper
1 tsp curry powder
1 tbsp vegetable stock powder
³/₄ cup frozen green beans
1 cup frozen peas
1.5 litres water
³/₄ cup vermicelli
1 cup frozen cauliflower
2 tbsp parsley, finely chopped

Batinjan Ma Lahma

[Bat-in-jan Ma Lar-ma]

Aubergine is a common component of Middle Eastern cooking. The key to picking the perfect aubergine is to squeeze it! If your thumb doesn't make an indent, the aubergine isn't ready yet. If it makes an indent which remains, it is overripe. If the skin bounces back, the aubergine is ready to be used in this warm and filling dish.

Created by Batoul Einja

serves 5 | 1h 15 minutes total time | 15 minutes prep time | 1 hour cooking time

METHOD

1. Remove the skin from the aubergines by cutting off the stem and peeling back the skin. Once peeled, cut the aubergine into slices about 2 ½ cm thick. Place the aubergines in a pan with the vegetable oil and fry over a medium heat. Set aside when done.

2. In a separate pan, heat some more oil. Add the diced onions and fry them over a medium heat until browned. Add the meat and once it has browned, season with the black pepper and salt. Add the chopped walnuts and parsley then stir well before taking the mixture off the heat.

3. Place another pan over a medium heat and add a small amount of oil along with the chopped tomatoes. Add the water and leave the sauce to boil, stirring occasionally. Once the sauce has come to the boil, take it off the heat.

4. Preheat the oven to 220°C. Line a casserole dish with the fried aubergine slices and layer the meat and onion mixture on top. Pour the tomato sauce over and put the casserole dish in the preheated oven. Leave to cook at 220°C for 30 minutes before serving.

INGREDIENTS

3 aubergines
1 litre vegetable oil
2 medium onions, diced
1kg lamb or beef, diced
½ tsp black pepper
1 tbsp salt
½ cup walnuts, chopped
½ cup parsley, chopped
800g tinned chopped tomatoes
½ cup water

This recipe can be served with rice and Aysha Alattar's delicious tabbouleh recipe (page 98).

Shish Barak

[Sheese Bah-rack]

Shish barak is a dish enjoyed across Syria, Iraq, Lebanon, Jordan and Palestine. Small parcels of tasty meat filling are cooked in a rich sauce, similar to its European equivalent, ravioli.

Created by Aysha Sharaf Jaafar

serves 5

1h 30 minutes
total time

45 minutes
prep time

45 minutes
cooking time

METHOD (for the dough)

1. Sieve the flour into a large mixing bowl. Add the salt. Slowly add the water and stir well until the mixture forms a dough. When the mixture has thickened into a dough remove it from the bowl and knead well, pushing it against a flat surface firmly with your hands. Repeat this process, turning and folding the dough each time. Then place the dough back in the mixing bowl, cover it with a cloth and leave it to rest in a warm place for 30 minutes.

METHOD (for the filling)

2. While the dough is resting, you can start on the filling. Add the oil to a pan and place it over a medium heat. Add the onion, salt and black pepper and fry until the onions have softened, stirring regularly. When the onions are soft, add the meat and stir well. Add the cinnamon, seven spice blend and pine nuts then fry the mixture until the meat has browned. When the meat is cooked through, take the pan off the heat and put it to one side.

METHOD (for the yoghurt sauce)

3. Place the dough onto a flat surface and flatten it out with a rolling pin. Cut the dough into small sections and roll each section into a ball with your palms. Take a rolling pin and flatten each ball of dough out into a thin circle. Put a teaspoon of the meat filling in the middle of each section of dough. To form each piece, fold the dough over the filling to form a semicircle, then fold the edges of the semicircle in on each other, pressing firmly to seal the filling inside.

4. In a clean bowl, mix the yoghurt and water together. Add the cornstarch and salt, stir well until all of the ingredients are combined, then pour the mixture into a pan and place it over a medium heat. Stir continually until it comes to the boil. Leave to simmer on a low heat for 10 minutes.

5. Place each piece into the simmering yoghurt sauce and leave to cook on a low heat for 30 minutes, turning occasionally. While the pieces are cooking, place a pan over a medium heat and add a little oil. Add the mashed garlic and fry for 2 minutes before adding it to the yoghurt mixture and stirring well. When the shish barak have finished cooking, serve with a topping of fresh coriander.

INGREDIENTS

for the dough:
500g plain flour
1 tsp salt
1 cup water

for the filling:
2 tbsp vegetable oil
1 large onion, diced
1 tsp salt
1 tsp black pepper
300g minced meat
1/4 tsp cinnamon
1 tsp seven spice blend
2 tbsp pine nuts

for the yoghurt sauce:
1kg plain yoghurt
1/2 cup water
2 tbsp cornstarch
1 tsp salt
2 cloves of garlic, mashed
pinch of fresh coriander, finely chopped

Mahashe

Mahashe is often served as a mixture of courgette, aubergine and green pepper stuffed with rice and meat. Although Busaina is from Idlib, mahashe is famously associated with Aleppo and is a particular favourite of her husband, Abdol, who originates from the city.

Created by Busaina Ismail and Abdol Kader Hijar

 serves 8

 1h 20 minutes total time

 20 minutes prep time

 1 hour cooking time

METHOD

1. Cut off the stalk end of the courgettes or aubergines, and deseed the pepper if using. Hollow out the middle of each courgette, aubergine or pepper and wash each one thoroughly.

2. Soak the rice in cold water for 15 minutes with a teaspoon of salt, then wash and drain it. Place the rice in a bowl and add a tablespoon of salt, along with the pepper, cumin and vegetable oil. Mix well. Add the minced lamb and half of the tomato purée to the rice and stir together. Stuff the courgettes, aubergines or peppers with the mixture so that half of each one is filled. Leave the top half empty.

3. Pour the water into a large cooking pot and add the remaining tomato purée with a pinch of salt. Put the pot on a high heat and leave the water to boil. Carefully place the stuffed courgettes, aubergines or peppers into the pot and cover with a lid. Leave to cook on a low heat for 45 minutes.

4. After 45 minutes, add the garlic and mint to the broth and leave the pot over a low heat for 5 more minutes. Remove the stuffed vegetables from the pot and pour the broth into bowls to serve alongside.

INGREDIENTS

1kg courgettes, aubergines or green peppers
1kg short grain rice
2 tbsp salt
1 tsp black pepper
1 tsp cumin
½ cup vegetable oil
200g minced lamb
4 tbsp tomato purée
2 litres water
1 tbsp minced garlic
1 tbsp dried mint

Layali Lubnan

[Loy-arl-ee Lub-naan]

Layali Lubnan (also known as 'Lebanese Nights') is a semolina-based dish which is well-loved across the Middle East. While it may be well known across the region, each country has their own unique take on the sweet, with some variations adding cranberries or cherries to the topping.

Created by Busaina Ismail and Abdol Kader Hijar

vegetarian

serves 5

1h 25 minutes
total time

1h 15 minutes
prep time

10 minutes
cooking time

METHOD

1. Mix the sugar and semolina together in a pan. Add the milk to the mixture and stir thoroughly. Put the saucepan over a medium heat and continuously stir the mixture until it becomes firm and thick. Once it has thickened, stir in the orange blossom water.

2. Pour the entire mixture into a deep, wide dish and leave it to cool at room temperature. When it has cooled, place the dish in the fridge for 1 hour.

3. After an hour, remove the dish from the fridge and pour the double cream and sugar syrup on top. Sprinkle the crushed pistachios over the pudding and serve by dividing into equal square portions.

INGREDIENTS

½ cup sugar
1 ¼ cups coarse semolina
1 litre whole milk
½ cup orange blossom water
1 cup double cream
¼ cup sugar syrup
1 cup pistachio nuts, crushed

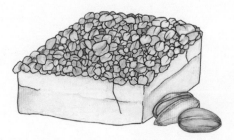

Mabrosha

[Mah-bro-shar]

This jam cake could easily be mistaken for a classic English dessert. Mabrosha is perfect for serving with your afternoon tea and the strawberry jam can be replaced with your favourite fruit preserve.

Created by Malak Albetare

 vegetarian   serves 5   45 minutes total time   30 minutes prep time   15 minutes cooking time

METHOD

1. Put the butter into a mixing bowl. Add the vegetable oil and sugar then whisk until the ingredients form a smooth batter. Add the first egg and whisk until it is well incorporated, then do the same for the other two eggs. Add the vanilla extract and whisk well.

2. Add the baking powder and one cup of flour. Fold them into the mixture until you have a smooth dough, then add the rest of the flour and stir it in.

3. Place the dough on a smooth surface. Cut off about a quarter and wrap it in cling film. Place this section of dough in the freezer for 10 minutes.

4. Preheat the oven to 180°C and lightly coat a baking tray with vegetable oil. Place the remaining dough on the tray, flattening it out to cover the tray. Spread strawberry jam over the dough.

5. Grate the frozen piece of dough over the tray, covering the layer of jam. Place the tray on the middle shelf of the oven and bake the mabrosha for about 15 minutes, or until the pastry is golden brown. Remove from the oven and leave to cool before serving.

INGREDIENTS

100g butter
¼ cup vegetable oil
¾ cup sugar
3 eggs
1 tsp vanilla extract
1 tbsp baking powder
3 cups plain flour
340g jar of strawberry jam

Remains of the pillar of
Saint Simeon Stylites,
North of Aleppo, 2006

Hama

Written by Walaa Ezzeldin and Ismail Al Rahmoun

The City of Hama ranks fourth in terms of population after Damascus, Aleppo, and Homs. It sits in the centre of Syria and is also the centre of Hama Governorate. It looks upon the Orontes River, and its weather is moderate and mild. The four seasons alternate there as is the case with the rest of the Syrian cities; the most beautiful of these seasons is the spring where the weather cools, landscapes bloom with flowers and roses, and greenery covers the plains and mountains.

No one can deny the historical and touristic importance of Syria. Its regions and cities are rich with monuments, mountains, summer resorts, beaches, beautiful nature, wonderful forests, and historical fountains which have no equivalent in any other part of the world.

Of these monumental sites, we must mention the Norias on the Orontes River in central Syria, which are the largest and oldest water wheels in history. Many of them still revolve on the Orontes River, forming a stunning and distinctive landscape. The beauty, magnitude, and uniqueness of these Norias prompted historians to call Hama the City of Norias, in addition to its other name, the City of Abi al-Fida, after one of its ancient kings.

Among the tourist attractions in Hama are Hama Castle and Al-Azem Palace, which is now the Folklore Museum. It is located in the centre of the old city of Hama in Al-Tawafrah. In the past, it belonged to one of the noble residents of the city, and today it contains many of the monuments and antiques that were found in Al-Asi Valley and the Citadel of ancient Hama.

There are many ancient mosques in Hama, such as the Great Mosque, the Nuri Mosque, and Abu al-Fida Mosque, as well as many ancient monuments and famous water arches on the Orontes River. Yet, if you go outside the city, there are many castles, such as that of the ancient city of Apamea, landscapes, mountains, and forests, as in Wadi El-Ayoun, Masyaf, Abu Qubays and Al-Laqbah, which are characterised by beautiful nature and mild weather.

Hama

The Spring Festival

An annual festival is held in the city of Hama during April every year, where citizens and tourists gather to watch beautiful folkloric shows and dances from all the Syrian governorates about ancient historical figures, with the Norias of Hama in the background welcoming guests with their remarkable sound. Along with the shows, theatrical performances and book fair, a popular market is held around the castle.

Kafr Nabudah

We come from the town of Kafr Nabudah, the bride of the Hamawi countryside. Its residents are known for their generosity, kindness, and chivalry. Today the population is around 25,000 but the town dates back to the Byzantine times; a mosaic dating back to the sixth century AD has been unearthed there. Al-Ashek Canal, which connects the cities of Al-Salamiyah and Apamea, passes through the town. Kafr Nabudah is famous for cultivating crops, the most important of which are potatoes, beets, and grains of all kinds. Some people in the town also depend on beekeeping, and on keeping cows and sheep. The town of Kafr Nabouda links the coastal region with the northern and eastern regions of Syria.

"Syrian people are proud of their food."

Walaa Ezzeldin, Ismail Al Rahmoun and their three sons, Mohammad, Ahmad and Hamza

Written by Rebecca Joy Novell

Walaa and Ismail are from Kafr Nabudah, a small village in the northwest of Hama. The people of Kafr Nabudah are very famous for farming and agriculture. "When we say Kafr, we mean farm," says Ismail. "I was raised as a farmer from my childhood on my family's land," he continues. "My father and my grandfather were farmers. I started work around six years old. My house was on the farmland and so you began working young. Of course I enjoyed it. My mother grew all the fruit and vegetables we needed at home. We would rarely go to the shops as we had everything we needed. The only thing we would go to the shop for was meat. Or if a vegetable was out of season and

we needed it for a special event, we would go to the shop."

"I used to have 150 boxes of bees to make honey. I used to have a lot of honey." Walaa interrupts to jokingly tell me that she has seen so much honey in her life that she doesn't need to see it ever again!

"All our family would live together on the farm," says Ismail. His seven uncles and father lived in the same place, and all his cousins grew up together. It is clear from the way they talk about home that they miss their way of life and the large, strong community they were part of. "In the village, you are all related and you all know each other," explains Walaa. "You could rely on your friends and neighbours to raise your children together. The children could play outside safely because you knew everyone."

When I ask Walaa why she chose to make halawat al jibn (page 87) for the book, she says that it was because it reminded her of her childhood. "I remember my dad used to bring this food from a special shop called Saloura Sweets in Hama. He used to bring it when we had guests from outside of the country to show them just how great Syrian food is."

Ismail tells me that "food means everything. Until now, I do not know any other type of food, only Syrian food. When I grew up, I saw my mother and mother-in-law cooking Syrian food and this is all we know. Syrian people are proud of their food. My three boys say their mum's cooking is the best in the world and the smell of Walaa's cooking reminds me of my mother and my childhood and all the stories that brings."

I ask Walaa and Ismail what it is like to eat food that reminds them of places and people that they miss so dearly. Ismail explains to me that "food is part of our culture. Yes, we came to the UK but we still need our food and our culture. Because we eat Syrian food daily, we are able to remember Syria daily. If we started eating different food, we may forget Syria and we never, ever want to forget. We need to remember our home and the happy memories we had. We need to remember Syria daily."

> "We need to remember our home and the happy memories we had."

Hummus

[Hum-us]

Hummus needs no introduction. There are hundreds of variations on this favourite dish, with each family adding different amounts of tahini and garlic to suit their own tastes. Hayat's mouth-wateringly good hummus is rich, thick and layered with extra tahini.

Created by Hayat Abouday

vegan

serves 2

15 minutes
total time

15 minutes
prep time

METHOD (for the hummus)

1. Drain the chickpeas. If you prefer a smoother hummus, you can remove their outer skins by pinching each individual chickpea until the skin slides off.

2. Put the prepared chickpeas into a blender along with the mashed garlic and lemon juice. Add the tahini and mix the ingredients together on a low speed until the mixture is thick and smooth.

TO SERVE:

3. Serve the hummus with a swirl of olive oil, a sprinkle of paprika, extra tahini and chickpeas if you like and a sprig of mint.

INGREDIENTS

for the hummus:
500g tinned chickpeas
1 clove of garlic, mashed
2 tbsp lemon juice
200g tahini

to serve:
olive oil
paprika
fresh mint

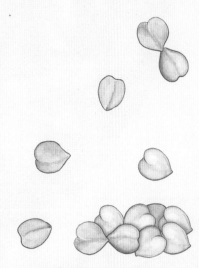

Fattoush

[F a h - t o o - s h]

Fattoush is a really simple, fresh salad. You can add any of your favourite fruit and vegetables to the salad. The key element is the toasted bread.

Created by Majd Al Majbel

vegan   serves 3   20 minutes   20 minutes
                             total time   prep time

METHOD (for the salad)

1. Wash all the vegetables well. Cut the lettuce into strips. Dice the cucumbers, green pepper, spring onions and radishes. Finely chop the parsley and mint, then put all the herbs and vegetables into a large bowl.

METHOD (for the dressing)

2. In another small bowl, combine the pomegranate molasses, lemon juice, olive oil, salt, dried red pepper and sumac. Stir the ingredients together well and then pour the dressing over the vegetables. Add salt to taste.

TO SERVE

3. Toast the Arabic bread under a grill and cut it into small squares. To serve, decorate the salad with the pieces of toasted bread.

INGREDIENTS

for the salad:
1 lettuce
2 cucumbers
$1/2$ green pepper
2 spring onions
7 radishes
1 bunch of parsley
$1/2$ bunch of fresh mint

for the dressing:
$1/2$ cup pomegranate molasses
$1/4$ cup lemon juice
$1/4$ cup olive oil
1 tsp salt
$1/2$ tsp dried sweet red pepper
2 tbsp sumac
pinch of salt

to serve:
2 loaves of Arabic bread

Pumpkin Jam

Despite being called jam, this recipe produces what we in England would refer to as a firm jelly. Unlike other Syrian sweet dishes, the sweetness of this jam is very subtle.

Created by Nasra Diab

| vegan | serves 8 | 9h 50 minutes total time | minimum 6h soaking time | 20 minute prep time | 3h 30 minutes cooking time |

METHOD

1. Peel and deseed the pumpkin before cutting it into small pieces, about 2.5cm cubes. Half fill a large mixing bowl with water. Add the pickling lime and stir well until it has completely dissolved. Add the pumpkin pieces and make sure they are fully submerged, adding more water if necessary.

2. Leave the pumpkin to soak overnight, or for at least 6 hours. Turn the pieces occasionally while they are soaking. When the pumpkin has finished soaking, remove it from the water and wash very thoroughly.

3. Put a large cooking pot over a high heat and add the two litres of fresh water. Let the water come to the boil before adding the sugar. Stir well until all the sugar has dissolved, then gradually add the pieces of pumpkin, stirring well as you do so. When all of the pieces have been added, let the water come back to the boil then reduce to a low heat. Leave the pumpkin cooking on a low heat for 3 hours, stirring occasionally, until the pieces become translucent.

4. Add the lemon salt and stir it in gently before taking the pot off the heat. Leave the pumpkin jam to cool completely before pouring the mixture into a glass jar and sealing with a lid.

INGREDIENTS

1kg pumpkin
100g pickling lime
2 litres water
1kg sugar
½ tsp lemon salt

Pickling lime is readily available online.

Shorbat Addas

[Shor-bat Ad-dass]

Majd's warming lentil soup is perfect for the colder winter months.
Created by Majd Al Majbel

vegan

serves 3

1 hour
total time

5 minutes
prep time

55 minutes
cooking time

METHOD

1. Wash and drain the lentils and rice thoroughly. Pour the fresh water into a pot, add the lentils and rice and put the pot over a high heat. When the water comes to the boil, reduce the heat and leave the mixture to simmer.

2. Add the stock cube, cumin and salt. Stir well and cook the mixture for 40 minutes or until it thickens and the lentils soften. Meanwhile, pour the oil into a clean pan and put it over a medium heat. Add the diced onion and fry until golden brown.

3. Add the onion to the soup and stir well for 5 minutes. Take the soup off the heat and pour into bowls to serve. Enjoy with toasted bread on the side.

INGREDIENTS

5 cups water
2 cups red lentils
1 cup short grain rice
1 vegetable stock cube
1 tbsp ground cumin
pinch of salt
2 tbsp olive oil
1 medium onion, diced
2 thick slices of bread, toasted

Mutabbal Batinjan

[Moo-tab-al Bat-in-jan]

This smoky aubergine dip is commonly served as a starter, along with hummus, chips and fattoush.
Created by Walaa Ezzeldin

 vegan

 serves 5

 35 minutes total time

 15 minutes prep time

 20 minutes cooking time

METHOD (for the mutabbal batinjan)

1. Wash the aubergines thoroughly and make a few small holes in them with a sharp knife. Place them on a baking tray and put them under a preheated grill on the hottest setting for around 15 minutes until the skin is blackened and the centre is soft. Turn the aubergine frequently to make sure it is blackened on all sides.

2. Leave the aubergines to cool for a few minutes before removing the stems and peeling off the skin, then put the flesh in a bowl and mash with a fork. Add the tahini, garlic and salt to the mashed aubergine and mix everything together.

3. Place a pan over a medium heat and add the olive oil. When the oil is hot, add the diced onion and fry until it turns golden, stirring regularly. Add the tomatoes and green pepper then reduce the heat. Leave the mixture to cook for 10 minutes, stirring regularly, before adding the chopped parsley. Save a little parsley to use as decoration.

TO SERVE

4. Fill a dish with the mashed aubergine mixture and layer the vegetables on top. Add the lemon juice and pomegranate molasses, stir everything together, then decorate the dip with pomegranate seeds, chopped parsley and olive oil to taste.

INGREDIENTS

for the mutabbal batinjan:
3 large aubergines
1/2 cup tahini
5 cloves of garlic, finely chopped
2 tsp salt
1/2 cup olive oil
1 medium onion, diced
2 medium tomatoes, finely chopped
1 small green pepper, finely chopped
1/2 cup parsley, finely chopped

to serve:
1/2 cup lemon juice
2 tbsp pomegranate molasses
1/4 cup pomegranate seeds

Djej Meshwi

[Dah-jej Mesh-wee]

Djej Meshwi, or roast chicken, is a common family meal that can be served for any occasion. It can be served with or without the rice and peas.

Created by Nasra Diab

| serves 6 | 1h 25 minutes total time | up to 6h marinating time | 10 minutes prep time | 1h 15 minutes cooking time |

METHOD

1. Before you start, preheat the oven to 220°C and wash the chicken thoroughly.

2. In a large bowl, combine the dried pepper flakes, bay leaves, salt and chicken seasoning. Mix well then add the vinegar. Stir until the ingredients are well combined. Add the vegetable oil, lemon juice and yoghurt and stir well.

3. Rub the marinade evenly all over and inside the chicken before wrapping it in aluminium foil and placing it on a baking tray. If you prefer, you can leave the chicken to marinate like this for up to 6 hours in the fridge.

4. Put the tray in the preheated oven and leave the chicken to cook inside the foil for 1 hour. After this time, remove the aluminium foil and put the chicken back in the oven for a further 15 minutes until the skin is golden brown.

INGREDIENTS

1 whole chicken
1 tsp dried pepper flakes
2 bay leaves
1 tbsp salt
1 tbsp chicken seasoning
2 tbsp vinegar
1/4 cup vegetable oil
1/2 cup lemon juice
1 cup plain yoghurt

Rice with Peas

Created by Nasra Diab

| vegetarian | serves 4 | 1h 15 minutes total time | 30 minutes soaking time | 5 minute prep time | 40 minutes cooking time |

METHOD

1. Put the rice into a bowl and cover it with water and 1 teaspoon of salt. Leave it to soak for 30 minutes before cooking.

2. Put a pot over a medium heat and add the ghee. When it has melted, add the peas and stir well. Add the remaining salt, black pepper and mixed spice.

3. Drain and rinse the rice and add to the peas. Add the 3 cups of boiling water to the pot and let it come to the boil. Reduce the heat and cover the pot with a lid. Leave the rice to cook on a low heat for 30 minutes before serving.

INGREDIENTS

2 cups short rice
4 tsp salt
2 tbsp ghee
1 cup frozen peas
1 tbsp ground black pepper
1 tbsp mixed spice
3 cups water

Knafeh

[Kuh-na-fah]

Knafeh is one of those desserts that will quickly become your new favourite guilty pleasure. Despite resembling a cheesecake, the flavour is closer to a freshly baked croissant. This recipe will create Knafeh in a pie shape. If you are feeling more adventurous you can make individually wrapped pieces such as those in the image to the left.

Created by Hayat Abouday

vegetarian

serves 5

12h 45 minutes
total time

12 hours
soaking time

20 minutes
prep time

25 minutes
cooking time

METHOD (for the knafeh)

1. To remove any excess salt, soak the mozzarella or akawi cheese in water for 12 hours before cooking. Make sure to refresh the water every 2 hours.

2. Add the sugar to the knafeh pastry and mix well. Melt half the butter and mix it into the pastry. Spread five tablespoons of ghee across the surface of a baking tray, making sure to go right into the edges. Place half of the knafeh mixture onto the tray, then cover it with a layer of grated cheese. Top the cheese with the remaining knafeh mixture, covering it with a thin, even layer.

3. Wearing oven gloves, carefully hold the edges of the tray over a medium flame, rotating occasionally to ensure each side is cooked evenly. Do not put the middle of the tray over the heat. Keep rotating the tray until the knafeh becomes golden. To check if it's cooked, press the mixture with a spoon: if it makes a crunching sound, it is ready.

4. Once the knafeh is cooked, turn the tray upside down onto a serving dish. Leave it to settle for 5 minutes before removing the tray.

METHOD (for the sugar syrup)

5. To make the syrup, pour the water into a pan and set over a medium heat. Add the sugar and stir well. When the mixture comes to the boil, add the lemon juice and boil for 5 more minutes. Then take the syrup off the heat and leave to cool. Pour the cooled syrup over the knafeh before serving.

INGREDIENTS

for the knafeh:
1kg mozzarella or
akawi cheese, grated
3 tbsp sugar
500g knafeh pastry
2 tbsp unsalted butter
250g ghee

for the sugar syrup:
1 cup water
2 cups granulated sugar
1 lemon, juiced

Hayat has provided a delicious pistachio filling as an alternative to the traditional cheese filling.

METHOD (for a nut alternative)

Add the pistachios, sugar syrup, sugar, ghee and water to a bowl. Mix everything together until it is combined well. Place the nut mixture where the cheese would be in the previous recipe. This can be placed in the oven at 180°C for 30 to 40 minutes until the top turns golden brown.

INGREDIENTS

for the nut filling:
1kg pistachios, crushed
4 tbsp sugar syrup
4 tbsp sugar
4 tbsp ghee
4 tbsp water

Halawat Al Jibn

[Hal-ah-wat Al Jibb-an]

Halawat Al Jibn proudly originates from Hama, although Homs often tries to claim ownership.
Once you take a bite of this divinely sweet dessert, you will understand immediately
why they fight over who created it.

Created by Walaa Ezzeldin and Ismail Alrmoun

vegetarian

serves 6

40 minutes
total time

20 minutes
prep time

20 minutes
cooking time

METHOD (for the halawat al jibn)

1. Place a pan over a medium heat. Add the water and sugar and stir well until the sugar has dissolved. Then gradually add the semolina, stirring continuously until the semolina is soft and the mixture has thickened. Ensure that you stir the mixture continuously in order to prevent lumps. Add the mozzarella cheese 100g at a time and stir it into the mixture. When all of the cheese has been added, keep kneading the mixture with the spoon until it becomes a thick, bread-like dough. Add the orange blossom water and continue mixing until the ingredients are well combined. Take the dough off the heat while you make the syrup.

METHOD (for the syrup)

2. Pour the water into a clean pan, add the sugar and stir continuously until the sugar has dissolved. Put the pan over a medium heat and when the mixture starts to come to the boil, add the lemon juice. Remove from the heat and put the syrup to one side to cool.

3. On a flat surface, roll out a sheet of cling film. Spread the cooled syrup evenly over the cling film. Place the dough in the middle of the cling film and roll it out into a rectangle about 3cm in depth. Wrap the dough in the syrup-lined cling film and leave it in the fridge for 15 minutes. After the dough has been left in the fridge for 15 minutes, take it out and remove the cling film. Spread the cream or sweetened mascarpone out evenly across the dough, then tuck one edge of the dough over and roll it up into a cylinder.

TO SERVE

4. Cut the roll into six equal pieces and decorate them with a sprinkling of ground pistachios and an extra drizzle of sugar syrup.

INGREDIENTS

for the halawat al jibn:
1 cup water
²/₃ cup caster sugar
1³/₄ cups fine semolina
400g mozzarella cheese, grated
3 tbsp orange blossom water
double cream*

for the syrup:
²/₃ cup water
3¹/₂ cups caster sugar
¹/₂ tsp lemon juice

to serve:
handful of pistachios, ground

* Double cream can be replaced by mascarpone cheese mixed with a little syrup to give an even sweeter taste.

The Norias of Hama on the
Orontes River,
Hama, 2007

Homs

Written by Intersar Arnous

If you may, I would like you to go with me on a journey through my home of Homs, a place full of delicious food and aromatic scents.

Our first stop will be in the popular market, and our first destination will be the perfumers store. You cannot come to Homs without visiting the perfumery stores full of smells. The smell of spices displayed side by side in the shops will interact with each other. The aroma will work its magic on you, and you will be a prisoner of those forever fragrant smells.

Our second stop is breakfast. Breakfast is one of the most important meals for the people of Homs, because all family members are present at the breakfast table. Breakfast contains various delicious delicacies, starting with olives and ending with a cup of tea. One of the most important items that should be found at the breakfast table is the most popular Fattet Hummus (page 162), followed by Al-Shanklish, Olives, Labneh, Ful, Chickpeas, Makdous (page 94) and Falafel (page 20).

Al-Shanklish is the master of the table and is made in the form of tablets by drawing cream from milk, adding spices, and leaving it under the sun to dry. After drying, it is left to ferment, so it is characterized by its musty smell and bitter taste. It is best consumed with hot tea.

Do you feel hungry yet? Now we will move to our third stop lunch. One of the most delicious, tastiest and most luxurious lunch foods is Kuba (Kibbeh) (page 31) in all types of fried, grilled, or prepared in the oven, and I cannot describe that feeling when you take the first bite of the kibbeh and it is hot and smells of fat. Kibbeh in particular has a special place in the hearts of the people of Homs because when you eat this meal all family members must be present, especially when we reach the most important part of the preparation, the grilling, when everyone stands near the charcoal grill waiting for the kibbeh.

Now to our fourth stop; after all this delicious and hearty food, we need a sweetener. The people of Homs are particularly creative with making many sweets and you can guarantee that every home will have at least one sweet dish in the pantry. Among the desserts famous in Homs, the sweetness of cheese, which is known by many of the shops of Homs, such as the shop of Abu Al-Laban and the chain of stores Al-Sawas, Al-Natour and others. The sweetness of cheese is a common food between Hama and Homs, and the two cities compete in adopting the innovation and development of this food.

We have in Homs a very special day for Sweets (Khamis Al-Halawa), which is a very old feast in the city of Homs. This feast coincides with the Thursday that precedes the Christian celebration of Easter. On this Thursday, the city is adorned with the bright colours of the sweets; storefronts, especially in the old market and the surrounding area, fascinate the eye with huge pink and white striped pyramids made from the sweet.

Last but not least, our final stop is the memories, our beautiful memories, which we dug in every street and corner in the two cities of Homs. We have everything in memory, and of course the memory is embodied in our food, because in every street in Homs you can listen and eat. For example, in Bab Al Sebaa, from the beginning of the street to the end, there are shops that sell food and sweets. You can eat a sandwich from the shop Abu Al Khair and visit the sweet shop Salora to have a piece of pie stuffed with walnuts. You can buy ice cream from the carpenter shop and if you wish you can buy Corn Aranis from the street vendor In the middle of the Bab Al-Sebaa neighborhood,

I hope you enjoyed our trip together today. Never forget to enjoy every step of your country.

To Homs, the capital of laughter. Thank you for your unforgettable memories.

The Legend of Homs

During our visits to the homes of Homsi families, we found that The Legend of Homs was a story that came up again and again. Homsi people are proud of this legend and it goes some way to explaining their reputation as 'comedians' or 'jesters'. Homs itself is known throughout Syria as the 'capital of laughing'. Mohamad Ekhwan told us the story in great detail and with great animation:

Several centuries ago, Homs was invaded by an army, believed to be the Mongols, who wanted to take over the land. The Mongols had a large and strong army and had already destroyed and occupied Aleppo. The Homsi people knew they could not defeat the Mongol army by might.

One day, the leaders of Homs opened the city's gates and welcomed in the enemy. The Mongols entered and found these older, respected men wearing their clothes backwards with pots and pans on their heads and earrings in their ears. They walked backwards and performed strange dance moves. They explained to the Mongols that the water from their river had made them this way and that anyone who drank from it would also become crazy.

The Mongol leader was fearful of his army becoming sick and so he immediately ordered them to retreat. The elders' silly behaviour is said to have saved one million people's lives. Legend has it that this retreat took place on a Wednesday and so until this day, Homsi people still celebrate 'Day of the Fool' every Wednesday.

I used to work in Syria growing fruit and vegetables

Rima Al Rasas, Fayez Al Moteb and their
two daughters Roaya and Maria

Written by Rima Al Rasas

I used to work in Syria growing fruit and vegetables. In 2011, I got married to Fayez and we had our first daughter Roaya while we were still in Syria. My husband worked in Syria raising horses. Shortly after she was born, we moved to Lebanon. Our second daughter, Maria, was born in Lebanon and so

I gave up work to look after the children. Fayez found work in Lebanon painting houses, growing flowers and working in a restaurant, until we were resettled in the UK. I have now returned to work and am employed in a local café in Lancashire.

Marwa and her children Yamen, Yasser, Thanaa

Rana Al Mogharbel, Mohammed Ekhwan and their children Nabil, Rama, Sara and Lara

Written by Rebecca Joy Novell

Syrian food is slow food. When learning the recipe for Kibbeh Hileh (page 123), I sat with Rana and her three daughters for over four hours, as we rolled tiny balls of bulgar wheat. We laughed about how this would never happen in my English house, where a four-minute ready meal is often too long a wait for food. Rana explained that Syrian cooking isn't just about the food you put on the table at the end of the day but about the experience you have making it. She described how the hours taken to roll the bulgar, would be done as a group, with female friends and family members using it as a chance to talk about things happening within the community; or in other words, food preparation is the perfect time for a good old gossip!

It is a labour of love for many mothers, a duty that they take very seriously. Rana told me that if all her family are not around the table, then she will not eat. Meal times are a time of unity and bonding. For Syrians, good food and strong families go hand in hand.

"Meal times are a time of unity and bonding."

Makdous

[Mack-doos]

This Syrian delicacy of oil-cured aubergines tastes sensational. Do not let the preparation time put you off as makdous can be made in big batches and will keep for up to one year once made. In Syria, families would traditionally make it in autumn, as this is when aubergines are at their best.

Created by Rana Al Mogharbel

vegan

serves 6

1 week
total time

1 week
prep time

1 week... 10 minutes
cooking time

METHOD

1. Carefully remove the stems from the aubergines and wash them well. Place a large cooking pot over a high heat and half-fill it with water. Let the water come to the boil before adding the aubergines, then place a small pan lid on top of the aubergines to prevent them from floating to the surface. Leave the aubergines to soften in the boiling water for about 10 minutes.

2. Remove the aubergines and place them in a bowl of cold water to cool. Once cooled completely, drain the aubergines in a colander. Place the colander over a bowl and cover the aubergines in the coarse salt. Place a small plate on top of the aubergines and weigh it down with a can, or any other heavy object. Leave the aubergines like this for two days to ensure that all the liquid has been drawn out of them.

3. For the filling, place the chopped walnuts into a mixing bowl along with the chopped red peppers and a teaspoon of salt. Stir well until the ingredients are mixed together.

4. Remove the aubergines from the colander and carefully open them by cutting a small line down the middle. Fill each aubergine with a spoonful of the walnut and pepper mixture, then place them back into the colander with the weighted plate back on top. Leave the stuffed aubergines like this for another two days.

5. After the two days, place the stuffed aubergines into sterilised sealable containers such as large jars and fill each container with olive oil so that all the aubergines are completely covered. Leave the aubergines in the sealed containers at room temperature for at least three days before serving. They are best served with warm Arabic bread. The stuffed aubergines can be stored in olive oil like this for up to a year.

INGREDIENTS

1.5kg baby aubergines
$1/2$ cup coarse salt
110g walnuts, chopped
500g sun-dried red peppers, chopped
2 litres olive oil

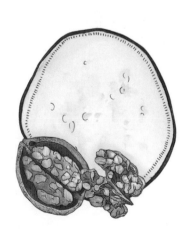

Muhammara

[Moo-ha-mar-ah]

Muhammara is a fresh tasting, thick dip which is best served with Arabic bread.
It can be eaten as a starter or as a side dish.

Created by Safaa Shoufan

vegan   serves 8   40 minutes total time   10 minutes prep time   30 minutes cooking time

METHOD (for the muhammara)

1. Put a pan over a medium heat and add water. Bring to the boil then add the bulgur wheat and leave it to cook for 20 minutes until it softens. Add the breadcrumbs and the chopped onion and stir well. Reduce the heat and add the pepper paste, tomato purée, pomegranate molasses, tahini, salt and cumin then stir the ingredients together. Rather than using a food processor to combine the ingredients, it is better to stir the ingredients thoroughly and press out any large lumps with the back of the spoon, or a pestle and mortar.

TO SERVE

2. Pour the dip into a bowl and leave to cool. Decorate with olive oil and walnuts.

INGREDIENTS

· for the muhammara:
400g fine bulgur wheat
200g breadcrumbs
1 small onion, finely chopped
100g pepper paste
100g tomato purée
150g pomegranate molasses
150g tahini
pinch of salt
pinch of ground cumin

to serve:
¼ cup olive oil
walnuts, as desired

Tabbouleh

[Tah-boo-lar]

The key to a successful tabbouleh is not only sourcing the freshest ingredients but also cutting the vegetables and salad as finely as possible. Tabbouleh is traditionally served with most dishes in Syria. At children's birthday parties, it is common to see tabbouleh and birthday cake served together.

Created by Aysha Alattar

vegan   serves 6   15 minutes total time   15 minutes prep time

METHOD (for the tabbouleh)

1. Boil the water and pour it into a bowl. Add the bulgur wheat and leave it to soak for 10 minutes before draining off any excess water.

2. In a large bowl, combine the chopped parsley, tomatoes and onion. Mix them together well before adding the chopped mint, lemon juice to taste, oil and salt. Add the prepared bulgur wheat and mix all the ingredients together.

TO SERVE

3. Place the tabbouleh in a dish and decorate with lettuce leaves and lemon slices.

INGREDIENTS

for the tabbouleh:
$1/2$ cup water
$1/2$ cup bulgur wheat
5 bunches of parsley, finely chopped
4 tomatoes, chopped
1 small onion, diced
1 tbsp fresh mint, finely chopped
squeeze of lemon juice
$1/2$ cup olive oil
pinch of salt

to serve:
handful of lettuce leaves
1 lemon, sliced

Mutabbal

[M o o - t a b - b a l]

Mutabbal is the same dish as Mutabbal Bathenjan, however Mona's recipe adds a layer of lamb for a different texture and flavour.

Created by Mona Al Shamiy

 serves 5

 1 hour
total time

 30 minutes
prep time

 30 minutes
cooking time

METHOD (for the mutabbal)

1. Wash the aubergines thoroughly and make a few small holes in them with a sharp knife. Place them on a baking tray and put them under a preheated grill at the highest setting for around 15 minutes until the skin is blackened and the centre is soft.

2. Leave the aubergines to cool for a few minutes before removing the stems and peeling off the skin, then place the flesh in a bowl and mash with a fork.

3. Add the yoghurt and tahini to the mashed aubergine and mix the ingredients together. Place a pan over a medium heat and add the olive oil. When the oil is hot, add the minced meat and the chopped tomatoes. Stir well then add the salt and black pepper. Reduce to a low heat and leave to cook for 20 minutes, stirring regularly.

TO SERVE

4. Fill a dish with the aubergine mixture and pour the meat and tomatoes over the top. Decorate the dip with the chopped parsley.

INGREDIENTS

for the mutabbal:
2 large aubergines
2 tbsp plain yoghurt
2 tbsp tahini
3 tbsp olive oil
500g minced lamb
2 medium tomatoes, finely chopped
1 tsp salt
pinch of ground black pepper, to taste

to serve:
1 tbsp parsley, chopped

Sfeha

[Sf-hey-ah]

This simple looking dish is actually more complicated than it seems and requires some time and patience. The dough is prepared in a very specific way but we promise you, it is worth the effort!

Created by Marwa Abu Shar

 serves 8   3h 15 minutes total time   3 hours prep time   15 minutes cooking time

METHOD (for the dough)

1. Sift the flour into a large mixing bowl. Add the salt, sugar syrup and baking powder then stir well. Combine the warm water and oil in a separate bowl. Gradually pour the liquid over the flour mixture, stirring thoroughly. Keep adding the water and oil and stirring the mixture until it forms a soft, stretchy dough. This can be done in a mixer if easier. Cover the dough with a tea towel and leave it to rest in a warm place for 1 hour.

METHOD (for the filling)

2. First, peel and chop the onions. Place them into a blender and process until smooth, then drain off any excess liquid. Place the meat into a deep dish. Add the salt, tahini, mixed spice, yoghurt, pomegranate molasses and onion purée. Mix all the ingredients together thoroughly. Leave the filling in the fridge while you roll out the dough.

3. Divide the dough into small balls, approximately 5cm in diameter, or the size of a large egg, and cover lightly with some of the ghee. Leave the balls uncovered for 1 hour.

4. After the resting time, flatten the balls until they are very thin rectangles, ideally 3mm thick. Brush both sides of the rectangles with the remaining melted ghee and fold each one in half, long ways. Place the ghee-covered dough pieces on a tray and leave for 20 minutes.

5. Stretch each rectangle as long as possible, ideally to 30cm long and 4cm wide. Roll the stretched dough back along itself into a cylinder, like a small pain au chocolat. Leave the dough to rest again for 30 minutes. Stand each cylinder on one end so the spiral on the bottom is placed on the surface. Press the top down to form a round of dough. With your fingers, press the round out flatter to create a small burger-sized circle.

6. Cover the dough circles with the meat filling and press firmly down. Sprinkle with pine nuts if desired. Lightly brush the sfeha with milk and place in the oven at 180°C for 15 minutes.

INGREDIENTS

for the dough:
1kg plain flour
2 tbsp salt
2 tbsp sugar syrup
2 tsp baking powder
$2^1/_2$ cups warm water
2 tbsp vegetable oil

for the filling:
3 medium onions
1kg minced lamb
1 tsp salt
2 tbsp tahini
$^1/_2$ tsp mixed spice
2 tbsp plain yoghurt
5 tbsp pomegranate molasses
$1^1/_2$ cups ghee, melted
$^1/_2$ cup pine nuts (optional)
2 tbsp skimmed milk

Yabrak

[Yab-rack]

Yabrak are stuffed vine leaves and a firm favourite at most community events. There is a vegan version called ylanji also in this section (page 107), so no one will miss out on these delicacies.

Created by Rima Al Rasas

serves 7   2h 30 minutes total time   30 minutes prep time   2 hours cooking time

METHOD

1. Remove the vine leaves from the jar and leave them to soak them in hot water.

2. Wash and drain the rice then put it in a pot. Add the fresh water and put the pot over a medium heat. Leave the rice to cook until it is soft and has absorbed the water. If the rice absorbs the water but isn't soft yet, add a little more water. When the rice is cooked, rinse it with cold water.

3. Put the prepared rice in a large bowl and add the diced meat, onion, salt, pepper, seven spice mix and two tablespoons of the vegetable oil. Mix the ingredients together until evenly combined. Separate the vine leaves and put a tablespoon of filling in each one. Close the leaves by rolling them into tight cylinders.

4. Put the remaining vegetable oil in a pot over a medium heat and add the lamb on the bone. Fry the meat until it is browned all over, turning occasionally.

5. Transfer the browned lamb into a clean pot, then spread it with the crushed garlic and arrange the stuffed vine leaves on top. Top the stuffed leaves with a little salt, lemon juice and a tablespoon of ghee. Pour enough water over the leaves and the meat so that nothing sticks to the bottom, then put a lid on the pot and leave it over a medium heat to simmer for 2 hours before serving.

INGREDIENTS

2 cups short grain rice
3 cups water
700g lamb, diced
1 medium onion, diced
2 tbsp salt
$3/4$ tsp black pepper
$1/2$ tsp seven spice mix (baharat or similar)
5 tbsp vegetable oil
1kg vine leaves, boiled
500g lamb, on the bone
2 cloves of garlic, crushed
lemon juice, to taste
1 tbsp ghee

Ylanji

[Yah-lan-jee]

The vegan version of yabrak: Safaa's ylanji ensures that everyone gets to taste the beautiful delicacy that is stuffed vine leaves.

Created by Safaa Shoufan

 vegan serves 8 1h 50 minutes total time 1 hour prep time 1h 50 minutes cooking time

METHOD

1. Before you begin, place the rice in a bowl and cover it with water. Leave the rice to soak for 30 minutes.

2. Put a cooking pot over a medium heat and add a glug of olive oil. When the oil is hot, add the onion and stir well until it begins to soften. Then add the tomatoes and peppers and leave the mixture to cook for 5 minutes, stirring regularly. Add the salt, parsley and mint and stir well. Then add the tomato purée, pomegranate molasses, coffee and sugar and leave the mixture to cook for 15 minutes, stirring occasionally.

3. After 15 minutes, add the water to the tomato mixture and wait for it to come to the boil. Drain and rinse the soaked rice, then add it to the pot and leave the mixture to cook for about 20 minutes, or until the rice has softened.

4. When the rice is cooked, take the pan off the heat and leave the filling to cool. Separate the vine leaves and fill each one with the rice and tomato mixture. Wrap the vine leaves around securely, ensuring the top and bottom are covered.

5. Slice the potatoes and lemon and line them along the bottom of a pot. Place the stuffed vine leaves over the potato. Add enough water to cover the vine leaves and place the pot on a high heat. Bring the water to the boil, then reduce to a medium heat and leave it to cook for 1 hour with the lid on. Make sure to check back frequently to see if more water needs to be added.

INGREDIENTS

1kg basmati rice
olive oil
1 large onion, chopped
1kg tomatoes, chopped
3 peppers (1 red, 1 yellow, 1 green), chopped
pinch of salt, to taste
100g fresh parsley, chopped
100g fresh mint, chopped
100g tomato purée
100g pomegranate molasses
1 tsp ground coffee
1 tsp sugar
2 cups water
800g vine leaves, boiled
3 white potatoes
3 lemons

The vine leaves can also be replaced with cabbage leaves.

Mandi

[Man-dee]

Yara's recipe adds a delicious twist to what is essentially a chicken and rice recipe. The mix of spices often leads mandi to be compared to a biryani. The chicken in this dish can be swapped for fish of your choice. Mandi is made for sharing and we recommend putting the cutlery down and getting stuck in with your hands.

Created by Yara Romia

 serves 7   24 hours total time   overnight marinating time   10 minutes prep time   2 hours cooking time

METHOD (for the marinade)

1. To prepare the marinade, combine all the ingredients in a large bowl then add the chicken and mix to coat it thoroughly. Leave the chicken in the fridge overnight to marinate, the day before you want to cook the meal.

METHOD (for the mandi)

2. After the chicken has been marinated, place it on a baking tray and cover with aluminium foil. Put the tray into a preheated oven at 200°C and leave it to cook for 2 hours.

3. While the chicken is cooking, place the rice in a bowl and cover it with water. Leave the rice to soak for 30 minutes. Meanwhile, place a pot over a medium heat and add a tablespoon of ghee and a dash of vegetable oil. When the ghee has melted, add the onions and stir until they have softened. Add the water, stock, salt, spice mix, cinnamon and turmeric. Stir well then let the mixture come to the boil.

4. Drain and rinse the soaked rice and then add it to the boiling broth. Put a lid over the pot and leave the rice to cook on a medium heat for 5 minutes before reducing to the lowest heat. Leave the rice to cook at this temperature for 30 minutes before adding the remaining ghee and vegetable oil. Stir these in, then dilute each food colouring in a little water and distribute the colours over different sections of the rice.

TO SERVE

5. Place the rice on a large serving dish and top with the chicken. Decorate with roasted almonds.

INGREDIENTS

for the marinade:
2 tbsp plain yoghurt
2 tbsp salt
2 tbsp tomato ketchup
$^1/_4$ cup vinegar
1 tsp ground cardamom
pinch of mixed spice

for the mandi:
2kg chicken
1kg basmati rice
$^1/_4$ cup ghee
$^1/_4$ cup vegetable oil
2 medium onions, diced
6 cups water
1 chicken stock cube
1 tsp salt
1 tsp mandi spice mix
1 tsp ground cinnamon
1 tsp ground turmeric
a few drops of red, orange and green food colouring

to serve:
handful of roasted almonds

Kibbeh Hileh

[Kib-eh Hill-eh]

Kibbeh Hileh is true, hearty, family food. Rolling the kibbeh balls is not a one person job and will require everyone to get involved. While it is a simple dish, which can be made from most of the pantry leftovers at the end of the week, we guarantee it will fill the family.

Created by Rana Al Mogharbel

vegan	serves 12	4h 10 minutes total time	2 hours soaking time	40 minutes prep time	1h 30 minutes cooking time

METHOD

1. Wash and drain the bulgur wheat thoroughly before use. Put the washed bulgur into a bowl and add one cup of water. Leave the bulgur in the water for 2 hours to allow it to soften. Put the softened bulgur through a mincer or food processor to ensure that it is soft and well combined before putting it back into the bowl.

2. Add the plain flour and another cup of water to the softened bulgar, a little at a time, and mix the ingredients together well until the mixture forms a dough.

3. Dust a flat surface with a little flour and place the dough on the surface. Break off small sections of the dough and roll them in your palms in order to form small balls approximately 2cm wide. Dust the balls with a little flour as you go along to avoid them sticking together.

4. Put a medium-sized pan on a high heat and add one cup of olive oil, all the onions and two tablespoons of salt. Fry the onions until they have turned dark brown, then set aside.

5. Pour the remaining two cups of water into a large pan over a medium heat and bring to the boil. Once the water has boiled, reduce the heat to a simmer. Carefully add the dough balls and leave them in the simmering water for 20 minutes. Once cooked, carefully remove the balls from the water with a small sieve.

6. Keep the cooking water and increase the heat in order to bring it back to the boil. Add one tablespoon of salt and the safflower to the water.

7. Place a clean pan on a high heat and add four tablespoons of olive oil. Add the dough balls and onions, stir well, then add the last tablespoon of salt. Leave the dough balls and onions to cook for 15 minutes, stirring occasionally.

8. Fry the garlic in a small pan with the remaining four tablespoons of olive oil until it turns golden, then add it to the large pot of water along with the lemon juice. Let the broth continue to boil for 15 minutes.

TO SERVE

9. Place the dough balls and onions on a plate and pour the broth into individual bowls.

INGREDIENTS

1kg fine bulgur wheat
4 cups water
1kg plain flour
2$\frac{1}{4}$ cups olive oil
9 medium onions, sliced
4 tbsp salt
2 tbsp dried safflower
9 cloves of garlic, crushed
4 lemons, juiced

Kapsa

[Kab-sah]

Kapsa is best served on one large dish in the centre of the table which everyone can share from. It can also be served with chilli and/or garlic sauce to give it extra depth of flavour.
Created by Souzan Sannoufi

| serves 4 | 3h 45 minutes total time | 2 hours marinating time | 45 minutes prep time | 1 hour cooking time |

METHOD (for the marinade)

1. To prepare the marinade, place the olive oil in a bowl and add the vinegar, black pepper and garlic. Mix well then coat the diced chicken with the mixture. Leave the chicken to marinate for at least 2 hours. Meanwhile, put the rice in a bowl with a teaspoon of salt and cover it with water. Leave it to soak for 30 minutes before cooking.

METHOD (for the kapsa)

2. Put a large cooking pot over a medium heat and add the vegetable oil. When the oil is hot, add the onion and garlic and stir well. Add the peppers and grated carrot, stir well until the vegetables begin to soften, then add the chopped tomatoes.

3. Add the salt, black pepper, curry powder, turmeric, cloves, cardamom and bay leaves. Stir well and leave the ingredients to cook for 5 minutes, stirring regularly, before adding the marinated chicken. Cook for a further 5 to 10 minutes, turning occasionally.

4. Add the water, dried lemons and stock and let the broth come to the boil. Once the water has come to the boil, remove the chicken and transfer it to a baking tray. Leave the broth on a low heat while you place the chicken under the grill on a medium heat, until it has browned on the edges.

5. Drain and rinse the soaked rice then add it to the broth. Bring the mixture back to the boil and add the sultanas. Reduce the heat and cover the pot with a lid. Leave the rice to cook on a low heat for about 20 minutes, or until it has softened.

TO SERVE

6. Divide the vegetable rice between individual bowls, or transfer to a large sharing dish, and top with the grilled chicken. Decorate with your choice of toasted nuts.

INGREDIENTS

for the marinade:
2 tbsp olive oil
1 tbsp table vinegar
1 tsp ground black pepper
1 tbsp mashed garlic

for the kapsa:
1kg chicken breast, diced
2 cups basmati rice
$^1/_2$ cup vegetable oil
2 medium onions, diced
5 cloves of garlic, finely chopped
2 yellow peppers, chopped
2 red peppers, chopped
3 green peppers, chopped
2 carrots, grated
3 medium tomatoes, chopped
1 tsp salt
1 tsp ground black pepper
1 tsp curry powder
1 tsp ground turmeric
1 tsp ground cloves
3 cardamom pods
2 bay leaves
2 cups water
2 dried lemons
2 chicken stock cubes
$^1/_2$ cup sultanas

to serve:
$^1/_2$ cup almonds or cashews, toasted

Okra with Rice

This simple okra stew, served over rice, is so easy to make. Beef can be added at the same time as the okra if you want to try a meat alternative.

Created by Bdour Sayoof

 vegetarian serves 4 1h 45 minutes total time 30 minutes soaking time 15 minutes prep time 1 hour cooking time

METHOD (for the okra)

1. Before you start, place the basmati rice in a bowl and cover with water. Leave the rice to soak for 30 minutes.

2. Place a pan over a medium heat and add the vegetable oil. Wash and dry the okra before adding it to the hot oil. Fry the okra over a medium heat for 10 minutes, stirring occasionally, before taking it off the heat. When the top of the okra begins to turn golden remove from the oil. Set to one side.

3. In a clean pan, melt the ghee over a medium heat then add the garlic. Stir well for 1 minute before adding the chopped tomatoes, stock cube, salt and pepper. Stir the mixture well and leave it to come to the boil before reducing the heat and leaving it to cook for 20 minutes. Add the okra and stir well.

METHOD (for the rice)

4. Place a large pot over a medium heat. Add the ghee and let it melt before adding the vermicelli. Stir well until the vermicelli turns golden. Drain the soaked rice and add it to the pot. Mix them together and leave over a medium heat for 4 minutes, stirring regularly.

5. Add the water, stock cube, salt and black pepper to the rice. Let the mixture come to the boil, then reduce the heat and cover the pot with a lid. Leave the rice to cook for 30 minutes.

TO SERVE

6. Divide the rice between individual bowls and top with the okra in tomato sauce.

INGREDIENTS

for the okra:
500ml vegetable oil
1kg okra
1 tbsp ghee
5 cloves of garlic, finely chopped
1 tin of chopped tomatoes
1 vegetable stock cube
pinch of salt, to taste
pinch of black pepper, to taste

for the rice:
1 tbsp ghee
2 cups vermicelli
3 cups basmati rice
6 cups water
1 vegetable stock cube
pinch of salt, to taste
pinch of black pepper, to taste

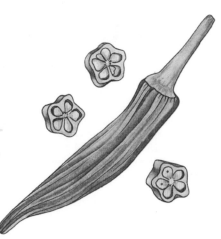

Sheikh Al Mahshi

[Shake Al Mar-she]

Sheikh al mahshi, simply put, is courgette stuffed with lamb, served in a yoghurt sauce. It's a favourite recipe across the whole of Syria. Different dishes of the same name can be found throughout the Middle East. In Lebanon, for example, the yoghurt sauce is replaced by a tomato sauce.

Created by Mona Al Shamiy

serves 5 | 2h 20 minutes total time | 30 minutes soaking time | 30 minutes prep time | 1h 20 minutes cooking time

METHOD (for the stuffed courgettes)

1. Before you start, place the rice in a bowl and cover it with water. Leave it to soak for 30 minutes, then drain and rinse before using.

2. Remove the stalk end of the courgettes. Carefully carve out the centres, removing the pulp. Wash the remaining outer layer well.

3. Place a pan over a medium heat and add the ghee. Once the ghee has melted, add the minced lamb and stir until the meat has browned. Add the diced onion and stir until softened. Add the parsley, stock cube, salt and black pepper before mixing everything together well. Take the mixture off the heat and leave it to cool.

4. When the lamb mixture has cooled, use it to fill the hollowed-out courgettes. Add a dash of vegetable oil to a clean frying pan and place it over a medium heat. Place the stuffed courgettes into the hot oil and fry until they turn light brown, turning them occasionally.

METHOD (for the rice)

5. Put the ghee and vegetable oil into a clean pot over a medium heat. Once the ghee has melted, add the vermicelli and stir well. When the vermicelli has turned golden brown, reduce to the lowest heat.

6. Drain the pre-soaked rice then add it to the vermicelli and stir well. Pour the fresh water over the rice and increase the heat to medium. Add a pinch of salt and black pepper then let the mixture come to the boil. Put a lid on the pot, reduce the heat and leave the rice to cook for 30 minutes, stirring occasionally and adding more water if necessary.

METHOD (for the yoghurt sauce)

7. Pour the yoghurt into a blender and add the cornflour with a pinch of salt. Mix the ingredients together on a low speed until they are well combined. Pour the mixture into a clean pot over a medium heat. Stir constantly until it comes to the boil, then add the stock cube and stir well. Place the stuffed courgettes into the sauce and leave to cook for 15 minutes.

TO SERVE

8. Divide the rice between individual bowls and top with the stuffed courgettes in yoghurt sauce. Decorate with chopped almonds if you like.

INGREDIENTS

for the stuffed courgettes:
2kg medium-sized courgettes
1 tbsp ghee
1kg minced lamb
3 large onions, diced
4 bunches of parsley, chopped
1 chicken stock cube
$1^1/_2$ tbsp salt
1 tsp ground black pepper
vegetable oil

for the rice:
2 tbsp ghee
1 tbsp vegetable oil
$1^1/_2$ cups vermicelli
$2^1/_2$ cups short grain rice
3 cups water
pinch of salt
pinch of black pepper

for the yoghurt sauce:
1kg plain yoghurt
2 tbsp cornflour
pinch of salt
1 chicken stock cube

to serve:
handful of almonds, chopped (optional)

Shakriya

[Shak-ree-yah]

Shakriya is a yoghurt soup which can be made with either lamb or chicken.
This simple, hearty meal can be served with either rice or Arabic bread.

Created by Marwa Kamall

serves 5

2h 35 minutes
total time

30 minutes
soaking time

15 minutes
prep time

1h 50 minutes
cooking time

METHOD (for the meat)

1. Before you begin, place the rice in a bowl and cover it with warm water and one teaspoon of salt. Leave the rice to soak for 30 minutes before cooking.

2. Put a cooking pot over a high heat and add the water and meat. Bring the water to the boil then reduce the heat to medium. Leave to cook for 30 minutes. As the mixture boils, a layer of foam will gather on the surface. Remove and discard the foam with a spoon as it appears.

3. Add the bay leaves, sliced onion, cardamom pods, cloves, salt and black pepper to the pot, then leave the mixture to cook for 30 minutes on a medium heat, then take the pot off the heat and remove the pieces of meat, leaving them to one side while you make the yoghurt sauce. Do not discard the lamb broth.

METHOD (for the yoghurt sauce)

4. While the meat is cooking, place the yoghurt into a clean cooking pot. Add the egg, cornflour and a tablespoon of salt. Whisk the mixture thoroughly, ensuring that all the ingredients are well combined, then place the pot over a high heat. Stir the mixture continuously until it starts to come to the boil. Take three cups of the lamb broth and add it to the yoghurt mixture. Stir well and allow the mixture to boil for 3 minutes.

5. Put another pan over a medium heat and add a tablespoon of ghee. When the ghee has melted add the mashed garlic and cook for 2 minutes. Then add the lamb, stir well and cook for another 3 minutes. Add this to the pot containing the yoghurt mixture and stir well. Let the mixture cook for another 5 minutes then take it off the heat.

METHOD (for the rice)

6. Place another cooking pot over a medium heat. Add the ghee and the vegetable oil. When the ghee has melted, add the vermicelli and stir well until it turns golden then reduce to a low heat. Drain and rinse the soaked rice then add it to the vermicelli and stir well.

7. Pour the fresh water over the rice and stir a little. Add the salt and black pepper and leave the mixture to come to the boil over a medium heat. Once the water has come to the boil, reduce to the lowest possible heat and cover the pot with a lid. Leave the rice to cook for about 30 minutes, or until it has softened.

TO SERVE

8. Divide the rice between individual serving bowls and top with the lamb and yoghurt sauce.

INGREDIENTS

for the meat:
2 litres water
1kg lamb, cubed
2 bay leaves
1 medium onion, sliced
5 cardamom pods
5 cloves
1 tsp salt
1 tsp ground black pepper

for the yoghurt sauce:
2kg plain yoghurt
1 egg
1 tbsp cornflour
1 tbsp salt
1 tbsp ghee
1 tbsp mashed garlic

for the rice:
2 tbsp ghee
1 tbsp vegetable oil
2 cups vermicelli
2$^{1}/_{2}$ cups short rice
5 cups water
2 tsp salt
1 tsp ground black pepper

Basbousa

[Baz-boo-sar]

Basbousa is also known throughout Syria as Hareeseh. Aysha's semolina cake can be served according to the below, or you can add rose water or orange blossom water to the simple syrup, creating something extra special.

Created by Aysha Alattar

vegetarian   serves 10-15   1 hour total time   40 minutes prep time   20 minutes cooking time

METHOD (for the sugar syrup)

1. First, make the sugar syrup. Pour the water into a clean pan, add the sugar and stir continuously until the sugar has dissolved. Put the pan over a medium heat, when the mixture starts to come to the boil, add the lemon salt. Add the ghee, stir well and then take the syrup off the heat. Leave to one side.

METHOD (for basbousa)

2. Crack the eggs into a mixing bowl and add the oil, yoghurt, lemon zest, vanilla extract and sugar. Mix the ingredients together until they are well combined.

3. In a separate bowl, mix the semolina, baking powder, shredded coconut, milk and salt together.

4. Combine the two mixtures in one bowl and stir thoroughly until everything is well incorporated. Leave the bowl to one side for 20 minutes. At this point, preheat the oven to 180°C.

5. Take a baking tray and spread the tahini across its surface. Pour the mixture over the top, ensuring that it is spread evenly across the tray.

6. Place the tray on the middle shelf in the preheated oven and leave the mixture to cook for about 15 minutes. Check that it is cooked through by inserting a knife into the middle of the mixture. If no mixture sticks to the knife when you remove it, the inside is cooked and the tray can be moved to the middle shelf of the oven to continue cooking until the top is golden brown.

7. Remove the tray from the oven and pour half the syrup over it. Leave the tray to cool completely and then pour over the remaining syrup. Cut the basbousa into even-sized squares and decorate them with a sprinkle of shredded coconut to serve.

INGREDIENTS

for the sugar syrup:
2 cups water
4 cups caster sugar
$1/4$ tsp lemon salt
1 tbsp ghee

for the basbousa:
3 eggs
1 cup vegetable oil
$1^1/2$ cups yoghurt
1 tbsp lemon zest
1 tbsp vanilla extract
1 cup sugar
$1^1/2$ cups semolina
$1^1/2$ tsp baking powder
$1^1/2$ cups shredded coconut
5 tbsp milk
$1/2$ tsp salt
1 tbsp tahini

to serve:
shredded coconut, as desired

Qatayef Asafiri

[Ka-tie-eff Ah-sah-feer-ee]

Qatayef is a delicate pancake, filled with a sweet creamy mixture and topped with pistachios.
These little desserts can be served with afternoon tea and are a perfect way to impress visitors.

Created by Rima Al Rasas and Fayez Al Moteb

vegetarian	serves 10	1h 50 minutes total time	1h 30 minutes prep time	20 minutes cooking time

METHOD (for the cream filling)

1. Pour the milk into a pan, add the cornstarch and sugar, and stir until dissolved. Place the pan over a medium heat and stir the mixture constantly until it thickens. Take it off the heat and leave it to cool before adding the cream. Stir the cream into the mixture and then leave it to one side while you make the pancakes.

METHOD (for the pancake batter)

2. Pour the milk into a large bowl. Add the flour, yeast, sugar and cornstarch then whisk the ingredients together until the batter is smooth. Leave the batter to one side for 1 hour to activate the yeast.

3. After the batter has been left to rest, place a non-stick frying pan over a low heat. Pour two tablespoons of batter into the pan and spread out into a small circle. Fry the batter on one side, until the bottom is golden and the top is full of bubbles. When the pancake is no longer shiny on top, remove the pancake and place it on a clean cloth.

METHOD (for the sugar syrup)

4. Pour the water into a clean pan, add the sugar and stir continuously until the sugar has dissolved. Put the pan over a medium heat, when the mixture starts to come to the boil, add the lemon salt. Then take the syrup off the heat. Leave to one side.

TO SERVE

4. Top each pancake with a tablespoon of cream filling. Using your finger, pinch the pancake closed around one side, leaving the top open. Garnish with lemon zest or ground pistachios. Pour the sugar syrup generously over the qatayef.

INGREDIENTS

for the cream filling:
2 cups semi-skimmed milk
2 tbsp cornstarch
$1/4$ cup granulated sugar
2 cups double cream

for the pancake batter:
3 cups semi-skimmed milk
3 cups plain flour
1 tbsp yeast
1 tsp granulated sugar
1 tbsp cornstarch

for the sugar syrup:
1 cup water
2 cups caster sugar
$1/4$ tsp lemon salt

to serve:
lemon zest
pistachio nuts, ground

Kleicha

[Klee-char]

Kleicha, not to be confused with Kleeja (known as Desert Candy), comes in many shapes and sizes. Bdourr's kleicha will remind you of good old tasty fig rolls.

Created by Bdourr Sayoof

 vegetarian serves 7 1h 25 minutes total time 1h 15 minutes prep time 10 minutes cooking time

METHOD

1. To make the filling, place the date paste in a bowl and add two tablespoons of melted ghee. Mix the ingredients together well until they form a soft dough. Shape the dough into 2.5cm long cylinders and leave to one side.

2. In a clean bowl, combine the flour, sugar, baking powder, salt, vegetable oil and the remaining ghee. Mix the ingredients until they are well combined and the mixture forms a smooth dough.

3. While stirring, pour the warm milk over the dough a little at a time. Mix the milk into the dough until it has been completely absorbed then set the mixture aside to rest for 15 minutes.

4. To make the adhesive mixture, add the egg white, milk and vanilla to a small bowl and mix them together until well combined. Leave this to one side for now and preheat the oven to 200°C.

5. Place the dough on a flat surface and roll it out into a rectangle of the same length as the cylinders of date filling. Cut the dough into pieces. To form each piece, place each section of filling at one end of a piece of dough, then roll the dough over to cover the filling. Brush each piece with the adhesive mixture and dip each one in toasted sesame seeds.

6. Place all the kleicha on a baking tray, then place the tray on the middle shelf of the preheated oven. Leave them to bake for about 10 minutes or until golden brown. Once browned, remove the tray from the oven and leave the kleicha to cool for a few minutes before serving.

INGREDIENTS

800g date paste
1 cup ghee, melted
4 cups plain flour
$^1/_4$ cup soft brown sugar
1 tsp baking powder
pinch of salt
$^1/_2$ cup vegetable oil
$^1/_2$ cup semi-skimmed milk, warmed
1 egg white
2 tbsp semi-skimmed milk
few drops of vanilla extract
3 cups sesame seeds, toasted

Krak des Chevaliers,
east of Tartus,
in the Homs Gap

Damascus

The Governorate of Damascus is home to the capital city of Syria, also known as Damascus, or as-Sam. The city of Damascus is steeped in cultural and religious history; it is referenced in the Old Testament of the Christian Bible. Indeed, Christianity is just one of the religions that still exist in Damascus, along with Judaism, Sufism and the Druze. The majority of the population follow Islam and the famous Umayyad Mosque, built in the 7th century, is one of the largest mosques in the world. The beautiful mosaic mosque is just one of the many heritage sites that have been damaged during the war.

"Nareen is extremely proud of her Kurdish culture."

Nareen Orfali, Mahmoud Sheikh Badr Eddin and their daughters Nourhan, Shilan and Fidan

Written by Rebecca Joy Novell

Nareen and her husband Mahmoud are Kurdish Syrians from the city of Kobani. Nareen is a full-time mother looking after her three highly intelligent and confident daughters. Two of them have already grasped perfect English. All three girls love their mother's cooking. Nareen's eldest daughter likes Kibbeh (page 31) and all her daughters adore Mahashi (page 60).

Nareen's husband was a singer back at home and fortunately has been able to carry on his singing career, performing all over England under the name Peyman Kobani. Nareen is extremely proud of her Kurdish culture. The Nowroz Feast is her favourite time in the Kurdish calendar. Nowroz happens every year on the first day of Spring, and is a time for all Kurdish people to gather together as families, celebrate and dance in brightly coloured clothes.

The Kurdish People of Syria

Written by Ahlam Hassan

Kurdish people are the largest group of stateless people in the world, with over 30 million Kurds living across Syria, Iraq, Iran, Turkey and Armenia. The Kurdish community is united by a common language, culture and race. For centuries, Kurdish people have been fighting for recognition and independence.

Kurdish people make up the second largest ethnicity in Syria. The majority of Kurdish people live in Northern Syria, in a region known as Rojava or Western Kurdistan, but they can also be found across Aleppo, Damascus, Hama and Homs.

Most Kurds speak Kurdish Kurmanji, however, prior to 2011 it was prohibited for Kurmanji to be taught in schools or spoken publicly, therefore Arabic is a common second language amongst Syrian Kurds.

For decades, human rights defenders have protested against the consistent harassment and discrimination of Syrian Kurds by the Syrian Government. Before 2011, you could be imprisoned for simply owning a Kurdish publication or playing Kurdish music and traditional

Kurdish dress was prohibited. Kurdish families were also not allowed to register their children with Kurdish names. Many Syrian Kurds were not acknowledged as citizens of Syria and were forbidden from owning property, accessing public health services or accessing higher education.

Syrian Kurds have played a crucial part in the battle against ISIS. The PYD or Democratic Union Party was founded in 2003 as a Kurdish political party. It is the PYD forces who have been responsible for defending the Rojava region of Syria from the Islamic State since 2015.

It is the Kurdish women of Syria, however, that have gained international attention, with the creation of the YPJ, or Women's Protection Units, in 2013. The YPJ is made up of approximately 24,000 all-female resistance fighters. These women continue to fight against the threat of the Islamic State. They were instrumental in the battle of Kobane and crucially, they have bolstered the rights and recognition of women in an area where women were previously overlooked.

Khaliat Nahal

[Ha-lee-at Nar-hal]

Khaliat Nahal, or honeycomb bread, can be filled with cheese or olives. These melt-in-the-mouth buns are sure to impress any dinner guest.
Created by Maha Barakeh

 vegetarian   serves 5   3h 25 minutes total time   approx. 2 hours proving time   1 hour prep time   25 minutes cooking time

METHOD (for the syrup glaze)

1. Start by making the syrup glaze. Mix the sugar, water and saffron in a pan then bring the mixture to the boil. The liquid will thicken after a few minutes. Once it has thickened, remove the pan from the heat and stir in the honey. Leave the syrup to cool.

METHOD (for the dough)

2. Combine the flour, sugar, yeast and salt. Mix them well then slowly beat in the egg, oil and melted butter. When they are thoroughly combined, add the milk a bit at a time, stirring constantly to avoid any lumps. Once the mixture has thickened, begin kneading it. While you knead the dough, add the water just a splash at a time, until the mixture is firm but soft. You may not require all the water. Continue to knead the dough for 15 minutes.

3. Place the dough into an oiled bowl, cover with a tea towel and leave the dough to rise for 1 hour until it has doubled in size. Once it has risen, remove the dough from the bowl and knead it lightly once more for 1 minute. Tear the dough into about 30 small pieces.

4. Take a piece of dough and stretch it out to make a small circle. Place approximately one teaspoon of cream cheese in the centre of the dough. Close the edges around the cheese to form a ball and seal the filling in. Repeat this process with the remaining dough.

5. Grease a cake tin with butter, then line it with the filled dough balls so that they make a honeycomb pattern with no spaces in between. Cover the tin with a tea towel and leave the dough to rise in a warm and dry place.

6. Preheat your oven to 180°C. Brush the surface of the dough balls with egg or oil, according to your preference, then sprinkle with sesame seeds. Place the khaliat nahal in the oven for about 20 minutes so that the surface turns golden. Remove the bread from the oven and pour the cold syrup glaze over the top while the bread is still hot.

INGREDIENTS

for the syrup glaze:
1 cup sugar
1/2 cup water
1/2 tsp saffron
1 tbsp honey

for the dough:
4 cups plain flour
3 tbsp sugar
7g instant yeast
1/2 tsp salt
1 egg
4 tbsp vegetable oil
4 tbsp melted butter, plus extra for greasing
1 cup semi-skimmed milk
1/2 cup water
225g cream cheese
1 tbsp sesame seeds

Patatas

[Pah-tat-a]

The spices in this recipe transform this seemingly simple chicken and potato dish into a fragrant delight.

Created by Sara Suheim

 serves 4

 8 hours total time

 6h 30 minutes prep time

 1h 30 minutes cooking time

METHOD

1. Before you start, massage the chicken legs with the apple cider vinegar and leave them to marinate for at least 6 hours before cooking.

2. After the chicken has been marinated, wash the pieces well. Take a large pot and put it over a high heat. Add the litre of water and the chicken and let the water come to the boil before reducing the heat a little. Add the salt, black pepper, chilli powder, ginger, cinnamon, curry powder, cardamom and bay leaves then stir the broth well. Leave the chicken to cook in the broth for 30 minutes.

3. Place the mashed garlic in a bowl and add the lemon juice along with a pinch of salt. Stir well then leave the mixture to one side. At this point, preheat the oven to 180°C.

4. Put a clean pan over a medium heat and add the vegetable oil. When the oil is hot, carefully add the potato slices and leave them to fry for 10 minutes. Then place the potato slices on a baking tray and sprinkle over the cumin, paprika, curry powder, all-purpose spice mix and a little extra salt and pepper.

5. Remove the chicken pieces from the broth and place them on the baking tray with the potatoes. Stir to make sure everything is evenly distributed.

6. Place the tray in the preheated oven and leave the potatoes and chicken to cook for 30 minutes. Take the tray out of the oven, brush the lemon and garlic mixture over everything then place back in to cook for a further 5 minutes. This dish can be served with either Arabic bread or rice.

INGREDIENTS

8 chicken legs
8 tbsp apple cider vinegar
1 litre water
1 tsp salt
5 whole black peppercorns
$^1/_2$ tsp chilli powder
$^1/_2$ tsp ground ginger
$^1/_2$ tsp ground cinnamon
1 tsp curry powder
5 cardamom pods
4 bay leaves
2 cloves of garlic, mashed
3 lemons, juiced
2 tbsp vegetable oil
8 potatoes, sliced into thin circles
1 tsp ground cumin
1 tsp paprika
1 tsp curry powder
1 tsp all-purpose spice mix

Ful Mudammas

[Fool Moo-dar-mas]

Ful is a popular dish across Arabic countries, with each country enjoying its own variation. In Aleppo, ful would traditionally be eaten as breakfast. Unusually, this dish is served lukewarm and should be accompanied by cold dips and bread.

Created by Alaa Shaaban

 vegan   serves 4   35 minutes total time   10 minutes prep time   25 minutes cooking time

METHOD (for the ful mudammas)

1. Put a pan over a medium heat and add all the fava beans including the water in the tins, and the salt. Stir well and bring it to the boil. When the beans have been heated through, remove from the heat. Add the garlic, lemon juice, cumin and pomegranate molasses.

2. Stir everything together, then add half of the tomatoes and a little of the parsley.

TO SERVE

3. Pour the ful into bowls and decorate with parsley and the rest of the tomatoes. Drizzle some olive oil over the ful and serve with Arabic bread.

INGREDIENTS

for the ful mudammas:
2 tins of fava beans (also known as ful beans)
1 tsp salt
2 cloves of garlic, crushed
2 lemons, juiced
1 tsp ground cumin
1 tbsp pomegranate molasses
3 tomatoes, diced
1 small bunch of parsley, chopped

to serve:
olive oil
Arabic bread

Ful medley or ful beans are available to buy in tins, often called 'Foul Madames' from any local Arabic supermarket.

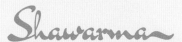

Shawarma

[Sha-warr-ma]

If you are not sure what to feed your children this weekend, shawarma will be an undoubted success with a winning combination of chicken and wraps. Feel free to add different sauces, salads and meats to your shawarma wrap.

Created by Ayat Abu Alijawz

| serves 6 | 4h 45 minutes total time | 4 hours marinating time | 15 minutes prep time | 30 minutes cooking time |

METHOD (for the shawarma)

1. Wash the chicken breast well, then cut it into thin slices. Put it in a large bowl and add the yoghurt, lemon slices, garlic, shawarma spice, salt, vinegar and vegetable oil. Mix the ingredients together so that the chicken is well coated. Leave in the fridge to marinate for 4 hours.

2. After letting the mixture rest in the fridge, take a baking tray and cover it with a little vegetable oil. Pour the chicken and its marinade onto the tray, spread out and leave it under the grill at 180°C for 30 minutes until the meat browns.

TO SERVE

3. Toast the flatbreads bread slightly, then fill each one with grilled chicken. Salad can be added if you wish along with mayonnaise or ketchup.

INGREDIENTS

for the shawarma:
2kg chicken breast
1 cup yoghurt
2 lemons, sliced
1 tbsp crushed garlic
1 tsp shawarma spice blend
1 tsp salt
$1/2$ cup white vinegar
$1/2$ cup vegetable oil

to serve:
6 Arabic flatbreads

Harak Osbao

[Hah-rack Uz-bow]

This vegan dish looks more like a work of art than a meal, but rest assured it is as tasty as it is beautiful.

Created by Ibtisam Hadifeh

 vegan   serves 8   3h 50 minutes total time   2 hours prep time   1h 50 minutes cooking time

METHOD (for the dough)

1. Sift the flour into a large mixing bowl. Add the salt and the oil and mix well. Add the sugar and the yeast and mix the ingredients together until well combined.

2. Gradually add the warm water, stirring until the water has been completely absorbed. Knead the dough for at least 5 minutes before shaping it into a large ball with your hands. Cover the dough with a kitchen towel or similar, then leave it to rise in a warm place for 1 hour.

3. After the dough has been left to rise, remove it from the bowl and place it on a flat surface. Roll it out into a thin circle then cut it into small, even squares 4cm by 4cm and dust each piece with a little flour, making sure the pieces do not stick together.

METHOD (for the tamarind sauce)

4. Place a large cooking pot over a high heat and add the water and the tamarind. When the water has come to the boil, leave it to cook over a medium heat for 30 minutes. After 30 minutes, strain the liquid into a small bowl, making sure to remove the pips. Use your hands to squeeze out every last bit of liquid. Set aside.

METHOD (for the lentils)

5. Place a clean pot over a medium heat and add the lentils. Cover the lentils with water and bring the mixture to the boil. Leave the lentils to cook for 20 minutes.

6. Before the lentils are fully cooked, add the tamarind sauce, pomegranate molasses and salt and stir well. Leave the mixture to cook for 10 minutes. Add the squares of dough, removing any excess flour and leave them to cook in the mixture for 30 minutes, again making sure you are always stirring the mixture.

7. Place a pan over a medium heat and add the olive oil. Add the finely chopped coriander and garlic and stir continually for 3 minutes. Pour the fried coriander and garlic into the lentil and tamarind mixture and stir continually for a further 5 minutes.

8 Place the pan back on the heat and add the sliced onions. Fry until golden brown then take the pan off the heat.

TO SERVE

9. Pour the lentil and tamarind mixture into a wide serving dish and decorate with the fried onions, Arabic bread and pomegranate seeds. You can also add extra coriander if you wish.

INGREDIENTS

for the dough:
4 cups plain flour
1 tbsp salt
200ml vegetable oil
1 tbsp sugar
2 tbsp yeast
1 cup warm water

for the taramind sauce:
2 litres water
500g tamarind, peeled

for the lentils:
500g red lentils
$\frac{1}{2}$ cup pomegranate molasses
2 tbsp salt
$\frac{1}{4}$ cup olive oil
1 small bunch of coriander, finely chopped
15 cloves of garlic, finely chopped
2 medium onions, sliced

to serve:
2 loaves of Arabic bread, cut into small squares
2 cups pomegranate seeds

Kebab Hindi

Kebab Hindi, or Indian Kebab, is not only delicious, but relatively healthy compared to many of the other recipes you will find in Syrian cuisine. Despite this, the combination of meatballs and tomato sauce makes it feel very much like good comfort food.

Created by Sara Suheim

serves 5 | 55 minutes total time | 10 minutes prep time | 45 minutes cooking time

METHOD

1. Put a cooking pot over a medium heat and add the ghee. Once the ghee has melted, add the onions and stir until they begin to soften. Add the chopped tomatoes and a pinch of salt and black pepper, stir well, then reduce the heat and leave the mixture to simmer.

2. Place the meat in a bowl and add the spice mix along with a pinch of salt and black pepper. Using your hands, mix the seasoning in well then form the meat into small balls.

3. Put a clean pan over a medium heat and add the oil. When the oil is hot, add the meatballs and fry them for 5 minutes until they start to brown. Then transfer them into the tomato sauce and leave them to cook on a low-medium heat for 30 minutes, stirring occasionally.

INGREDIENTS

1 tbsp ghee
2 large onions, chopped
2 tins of chopped tomatoes
2 tsp salt
2 tsp ground black pepper
1kg minced beef or lamb
1 tsp all-purpose spice mix
1 tbsp vegetable oil

This dish is best served with rice.

Kharshouf

Kharshouf is a common mealtime dish in any Syrian home. While it is most commonly served with beef, Maha has provided a delicious vegetarian alternative as well.

Created by Maha Barakeh

Beef

 serves 7
 1h 20 minutes total time
20 minutes prep time
 1 hour cooking time

METHOD

1. Place a large cooking pot over a high heat and half-fill it with water. Leave the water to come to the boil before carefully adding the artichokes. Add the salt and lemon juice and leave the artichokes to boil for about 5 minutes, then remove them from the pot.

2. Place a pan over a medium heat, then add the olive oil. When the oil is hot, add the artichokes and fry until they start to turn golden brown, turning occasionally. Place the artichokes on a plate to cool.

3. Place a clean pan over a medium heat and add the ghee. Once the ghee has melted, add the diced onion and stir for 5 minutes until the onion has softened. Then add the minced meat and stir for another 10 minutes, until it has begun to brown. Add a teaspoon of salt along with the black pepper and mixed spice and stir well before taking the meat mixture off the heat.

4. Preheat the oven to 180°C and lightly cover a baking tray with a little ghee. Carefully peel the artichokes apart and fill each one with the meat mixture, being sure to fill them between the leaves. Place the stuffed artichoke pieces into a roasting tin and pour the cup of water in. Cover the tray with aluminium foil then place it on the middle shelf of the oven for 15 minutes. Remove the tray from the oven and serve the stuffed artichoke pieces with rice or Arabic bread.

INGREDIENTS

15 artichokes
$1^1/_2$ tbsp salt
1 tsp lemon juice
1 tbsp olive oil
1 tbsp ghee
1 medium onion, diced
250g minced beef
$^1/_2$ tsp ground black pepper
$^1/_2$ tsp mixed spice
1 cup water

Vegetarian

 vegetarian
serves 7
1h 20 minutes total time
20 minutes prep time
 1 hour cooking time

METHOD

1. Place a large cooking pot over a high heat and half-fill it with water. Leave the water to come to the boil before carefully adding the artichokes. Add the salt and lemon juice and leave the artichokes to boil for about 5 minutes, then remove them from the pot.

2. Take a pan and place it over a medium heat, then add half of the olive oil. When the oil is hot, add the artichoke pieces and fry them until they are golden brown, turning occasionally. Then place the pieces of artichoke on a plate to cool.

3. To make the bechamel sauce, add the oil and ghee to a saucepan and place the pan over a low heat. Once the ghee has melted, start gradually adding the flour. Stir constantly until the flour has been completely absorbed by the oil and ghee. Reduce the hob to the lowest possible heat and start to add the milk slowly. Stir the mixture as you add the milk, little by little. Once all of the milk has been added and the ingredients are well combined, add the salt and black pepper. Keep stirring the mixture until it forms a smooth sauce, then take it off the heat.

4. Place a clean pan over a medium heat and add the remaining olive oil. Add the diced onions and stir for 5 minutes until the onion is golden. Add the carrots and mushrooms and stir until the vegetables have softened, then add the peas and stir well. Pour half of the bechamel sauce over the vegetables and stir until all the ingredients are well combined, then take the mixture off the heat.

5. Preheat the oven to 180°c and lightly cover a baking tray with a little ghee. Carefully peel the artichokes apart and fill each one with the vegetable and bechamel mixture, being sure to fill them between the leaves. Place the stuffed artichoke pieces into a roasting tin and pour the cup of water in. Cover the tray with aluminium foil then place it on the middle shelf of the oven for 15 minutes. Remove the tray from the oven and serve the stuffed artichoke pieces with the remaining bechamel sauce and rice or Arabic bread.

INGREDIENTS

15 artichokes
1 tbsp salt
1 tsp lemon juice
2 tbsp olive oil
1 medium onion, diced
2 medium carrots, cubed
handful of mushrooms, sliced
1 cup frozen peas
1 tbsp ghee
1 cup water

for the bechamel sauce:
3 tbsp olive oil
3 tbsp ghee
5 tbsp plain flour
1 litre whole milk
2 tsp salt
1 tsp ground black pepper

Balouza

[Bah-loo-zar]

Balouza recipes are passed down through the generations in Syria, meaning that there are many different variations of this refreshing homemade dessert. Its common features are a distinctive orange flavour and satisfying layered appearance.

Created by Ibtisam Hadifeh

| vegetarian | serves 4 | 5 hours total time | 4 hours prep time | 1 hour cooking time |

METHOD (for the base layer)

1. Pour the milk into a pan and add the cornflour. Stir well until the cornflour has dissolved into the milk. Add the sugar and stir well. Put the mixture over a medium heat and stir constantly. When the mixture starts to come to the boil, add the vanilla extract. Continue stirring the mixture until the vanilla is well combined, then take the pan off the heat.

2. Pour the mixture into small bowls until each one is half full. Leave the base layer to cool at room temperature before putting the bowls in the fridge to chill and set.

METHOD (for the top layer)

3. Pour the orange juice into a clean pan. Add the cornflour and stir well until it has dissolved into the orange juice, then stir in the sugar.

4. Put the pan over a medium heat and stir the mixture continuously until it thickens. When the mixture has thickened, take it off the heat and leave it to cool at room temperature.

5. Take the bowls out of the fridge and pour the thick orange mixture over the milk layer until each bowl is full. Decorate them with orange slices, then leave each bowl in the fridge for 3 hours before serving.

INGREDIENTS

for the base layer:
4 cups whole milk
4 tbsp cornflour
6 tbsp granulated sugar
1 tbsp vanilla extract

for the top layer:
3 cups fresh orange juice
3 tbsp cornflour
$4^1/_2$ tbsp granulated sugar
1 medium orange, sliced

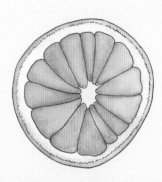

Muhallabia

[Moo-har-lar-bee-ar]

Muhallabia is one of the oldest Damascene dishes still eaten today. Sweet milk contrasts with savoury nuts in this dessert that can be enjoyed by children and adults alike. It is typically served on special occasions, such as weddings or engagement parties.

Created by Alaa Shaaban

 vegetarian

 serves 6

 2h 30 minutes total time

 2h 15 minutes prep time

 15 minutes cooking time

METHOD (for the muhallabia)

1. In a large bowl, mix the milk and cornstarch together. Stir well until the cornstarch dissolves then add the rose water, orange blossom water, cream, vanilla extract and sugar. Mix everything together until well combined.

2. Pour the mixture into a cooking pot and put it over a medium heat. Stir the mixture continuously as it comes to the boil. When it has boiled, keep stirring the mixture on the heat until it becomes thick. Taste the mixture and add more sugar as desired.

3. When the mixture has thickened, pour it into six individual glass jars and leave to cool at room temperature. Leave the glasses in the fridge for at least 2 hours before serving.

TO SERVE

4. Decorate each dessert with chopped pistachios and almonds or cashews, as preferred, with some tinned cherries to finish if you like.

INGREDIENTS

for the muhallabia:
4 cups whole milk
6 tbsp cornstarch
$^1/_2$ cup rose water
$^1/_2$ cup orange blossom water
1 cup fresh double cream
1 tsp vanilla extract
4 tsp sugar

to serve:
handful of pistachios, chopped
handful of almonds or cashews, chopped
1 tin of cherries (optional)

Aish Al Bolbol

[Eysh Al Bolbol]

Making aish al bolbol, the 'nightingale's nest', is a sure way to impress guests.
These delicate little pistachio bites are a favourite in Damascus.
Created by Ayat Abo Aljawz

 vegetarian   serves 6   45 minutes total time   15 minutes prep time   30 minutes cooking time

METHOD (for the aish al bolbol)

1. Before you begin, preheat the oven to 150°C. In a small pan, melt the ghee over a low heat, stirring occasionally. Once melted, take it off the heat.

2. To form each piece, break off a small section of shredded Kataifi pastry and form it into a circular bird's nest shape, leaving an empty space in the middle of each one. Brush each piece with a little of the melted ghee, then place a spoonful of ground pistachios in the middle of each piece and lightly cover the nuts with ghee.

3. Place the filled pastries on a baking tray and leave the tray on the middle shelf of the preheated oven for 25 minutes, or until the pastry is golden brown.

METHOD (for the syrup)

4. Pour the water into a clean pan, add the sugar and stir continuously until the sugar has dissolved. Put the pan over a medium heat and when the mixture starts to come to the boil, add the lemon juice. Then take the syrup off the heat. Leave to one side.

TO SERVE

5. Pour the syrup over the baked aish al bolbol.

INGREDIENTS

for the aish al bolbol:
1 tbsp ghee
1/2 packet kataifi pastry, shredded
2 cups pistachio nuts, ground

for the syrup:
1 cup water
2 1/4 cups caster sugar
1 1/2 tsp lemon juice

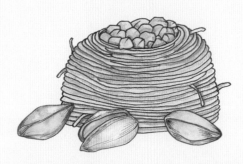

The Umayyad Mosque,
Damascus

Daraa

written by Ahmad Al Abboud

"Hauran, Hauran is a paradise." This is how the people from my city, Daraa, sing about the area we originate from. And it is indeed a paradise, and has always been throughout history. Hauran, a region that spans southern Syria, was called the 'Silo of Rome' because it provided the Roman Empire with its famous, internationally recognised wheat. Daraa or Zaraa, as it is called by the villagers, is located on a low plain, making its climate suitable for many different crops, and the city has gained fame from many of its fruit and vegetables, including tomatoes. Agriculture is a major part of our way of life in Daraa, and shaped my own family. I am one of 11 siblings: six girls and five boys. Having big families is the norm in our region, as the agricultural work requires many hands.

Our family was not only made up of 11 people, but also 11 different temperaments and 11 different ways of thinking! Fortunately, the one thing that united us was food. Food ensured that we gathered together as a family, daily. Food led to discussions and conversations around the table, where every topic you can think of was discussed and everyone participated. Ultimately for my family, food created unforgettable memories.

For example, before or after Friday prayer, which is a sacred day for all Muslims, you could hear the sound of sizzling ghee coming through open windows from kitchens while you walked along the street. Once we had returned home, after the prayer, we often had a malihi dish, which required the collaborative effort of all the family to prepare. Sometimes, we had haurani pies, which my mother excelled at making and was famous for. On days of Eid, after the Eid prayer and after visiting the graves of our dead relatives, our family, like most others, would gather around to eat a hearty breakfast, which consisted of haurani pies, tomato juice, and ayran drink, made from yoghurt. These, for me, are unforgettable moments.

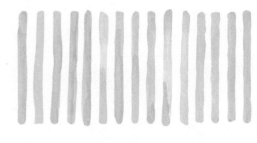

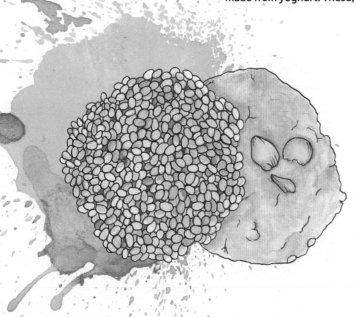

Daraa

Like any family in this scary world, my wife, children and I were dreaming of a happy life and building a beautiful future for ourselves in Daraa. Yet war erupted in our country, destroying all those beautiful dreams and the hopes we had nurtured. It turned life in Syria into a living hell and so we had to leave our house and our dreams behind, burning in the fires of war, and head towards an unknown future as refugees.

After fleeing to Jordan, we began a new journey of suffering and deprivation in the asylum camps. However, we didn't give up. We tried to build a life despite all the difficulties, exhaustion, oppression and homesickness. Amidst all the cruel circumstances that we faced in Jordan, we received a call from the UN, and that was a turning point in our life. It was the first step on our path to this beautiful country, England, which has given us the safety and warmth that we lost in our homeland. And despite our grief, we are so grateful for the decent, safe life that this country has provided for us and our children.

"Even the simple things are such beautiful memories

Balqis Faroukh, Inad Al Hamdan and their sons, Yousef and Jad

Written by Rebecca Joy Novell

Balqis left Daraa when she was just 16 years old. Despite her young age, she still vividly remembers her way of life in Syria. "I still remember each and every time I spent with my relatives. Even the simple things are such beautiful memories now. I used to go with my mum to visit my uncles and aunties and we would spend hours at their house, just telling jokes and enjoying each other's company. I still remember sitting with my neighbours in front of our houses as we would share our dreams and our secrets. I remember my friends who I thought I would always grow up with, and the school we went to. Often, I think about how when I left that school, I left my dreams there too." At 16, Balqis was forced to move to a refugee camp in Lebanon where she lived for four years. During that time, she got married and had her first son, Yousef. Jad was born in England, after the family resettled in the UK. Balqis now has dreams of becoming a police officer.

"My family are my strength in this country"

Wahiba Al Barakat, Diab Faorukh and their children Ghayth and Hajar

Written by Balqis Faroukh (Wahiba and Diab's daughter)

I will tell you about my family. I am one of Wahiba and Diab's daughters, and I have two sisters and four brothers. We spent our childhood growing up in Syria in the same house. We were brought up to be loving and understanding towards one other. My father is a very understanding man. My mother and father are the most encouraging people I know. They are always supporting me to do what I love and they have taught me not to allow anyone to tell me I am not capable of achieving my dreams.

I now live in Britain with my beautiful family: my husband and my children, Youssef and Jad. My parents and brothers are in another house in the same town. My father tells me every day that he does not feel that the day was beautiful if myself and my children do not go to visit him. My children are very attached to their grandparents. They treat my children as if they were their own.

My family are my strength in this country. My sisters are the kindest and most beautiful girls in this world and they are always asking God the best for me. My brothers are my life; the beating of my heart, and the air that I breathe is nothing without them. They are so affectionate with my children. My children love their uncles very much and shout with joy when they come to visit us. My other sister is still in Lebanon, living in difficult circumstances. It makes me very sad when I see my mother and father worrying about her. They are always thinking of their children. We all know how lucky we are to have parents as wonderful as them.

Juz Muz

[Juhz-muhz]

With a name this wonderful, you know the food will be fantastic! Juz muz may also be referred to as shakshuka. Put simply, it's fried eggs in a spicy tomato sauce and it's perfect when you need a breakfast that will keep you going all morning.

Created by Malak Al Betare

vegetarian

serves 4

20 minutes total time

5 minutes prep time

20 minutes cooking time

METHOD (for the juz muz)

1. Put a pan over a medium heat and add the olive oil. When the oil is hot, add the diced onion. Add the salt and pepper and stir well until the onions are golden.

2. Now add the chopped tomatoes, mixed spice and curry powder. Stir the mixture well then reduce the heat a little. Move the tomato sauce to the sides of the pan, creating a space in the middle. Break the eggs into the space in the middle of the pan and add a pinch of salt.

3. Place a lid over the pan and leave on a low heat until the eggs are cooked to your liking.

TO SERVE

4. Decorate with chopped parsley to serve.

INGREDIENTS

for the juz muz:
3 tbsp olive oil
1 medium onion, diced
$1^1/_2$ tsp salt
$^1/_2$ tsp ground black pepper
2 tins of chopped tomatoes
1 tsp mixed spice
1 tsp curry powder
4 eggs

to serve:
1 tbsp parsley, finely chopped

Fatayer

[Fat-eye-ah]

Fatayer is the Arabic equivalent of pizza. It can be served in many shapes and sizes. Lebanese fatayer is closer to an open Cornish pasty in appearance. Mona's fatayer is a large, thin, circular version served at the most special occasions, including weddings and Eid.

Created by Mona Al Hamadi

 serves 8

 2h 5 minutes total time

 1h 20 minutes prep time

 45 minutes cooking time

METHOD (for the dough)

1. Sift the flour into a large mixing bowl. Add the salt, instant yeast and sugar then mix the ingredients together. Gradually add the water, stirring continuously. Keep adding the water slowly until it is well combined with the other ingredients.

2. Knead the dough well with your palms, then shape it into a large ball. Cover the ball of dough evenly with the olive oil, then cover it with a kitchen towel or similar and leave it to rest in a warm place for 40 minutes.

METHOD (for the filling)

3. Place a pot over a medium heat and add the ghee. Once the ghee has melted, add the diced onions and stir for 2 minutes. Add the minced meat, salt and black pepper then stir well. Leave the lamb to cook for 10 minutes, stirring regularly. Add the chopped tomatoes to the pot and stir well, then leave the mixture to cook for 20 minutes.

4. Whilst the lamb is cooking, preheat the oven to 250°C. Once the dough has risen, separate it into equally sized balls and leave them to rest for another 20 minutes. Dust a flat surface with a little flour and roll one of the dough balls out into a flat circle, making sure it is the same size as the tray you are using. Place three tablespoons of the filling in the centre. Roll another dough ball out flat and use this piece of dough to cover the filling, pressing down firmly so that the filling is spread across the fatayer. Press on each edge to seal the fatayer. Repeat this process with the remaining dough until all of the filling has been used up.

5. Once you have formed the fatayer, place them on a baking tray. Place the tray on the middle shelf of the preheated oven and bake for 10 to 15 minutes until they are golden brown. Remove the tray from the oven and lightly cover the fatayer with olive oil. Leave the fatayer to cool for a few minutes before serving.

INGREDIENTS

for the dough:
1kg plain flour
1 tsp salt
1^1/$_2$ tbsp instant yeast
1 tbsp granulated sugar
2^1/$_2$ cups warm water
1 tbsp olive oil

for the filling:
1 tbsp ghee
5 medium onions, diced
1kg minced lamb
1 tbsp salt
1 tbsp ground black pepper
2 tins of chopped tomatoes

Fattet Hummus

[Fat-et Hum-us]

Malak's fattet hummus is a breakfast that will give you enough energy for the whole day. This quick and easy dish is best served immediately to stop the bread from becoming soggy.

Created by Malak Al Betare

vegetarian   serves 5   20 minutes total time   15 minutes prep time   5 minutes cooking time

METHOD (for the chickpeas)

1. Preheat the oven to 180°C and cut the bread into 5cm squares. Cover the bread with a little bit of olive oil. Cook the bread until golden brown and toasted on both sides. Place the chickpeas, two cups of water, salt and cumin into a pan and heat gently.

METHOD (for the fatta sauce)

2. Place the hummus in a bowl and add the tahini, lemon juice, yoghurt, one teaspoon of salt, cumin and half the garlic. Mix together well. Add three ladles of the chickpea water to the mixture and stir well.

3. In another bowl, combine three ladles of the chickpea water with a pinch of salt and the remaining garlic, then pour it over the toasted bread.

4. Pour half of the fatta sauce over the soaked bread and stir everything together well. Place two ladles of chickpeas into the bowl and stir thoroughly.

5. Cover the mixture with the remaining chickpeas, then pour the remaining fatta sauce over the chickpeas until it covers them.

TO SERVE

6. Scatter the pomegranate seeds, pine nuts and red pepper over the top for decoration. Heat the ghee until it is sizzling hot and drizzle over the top to finish.

INGREDIENTS

for the chickpeas:
2 portions of Arabic bread, toasted
2 tbsp olive oil
500g chickpeas, cooked
2 cups of water
1 tbsp salt
1 tbsp cumin

for the fatta sauce:
300ml smooth hummus
$^1/_2$ cup tahini
$^1/_2$ cup lemon juice
4 tbsp plain yoghurt
2 tsp salt
pinch of cumin
2 tsp crushed garlic

to serve:
1 pomegranate
2 tsp pine nuts
1 dried red pepper
3 tbsp ghee

It can easily be made into a vegan dish by replacing the yoghurt with a non-dairy alternative or more hummus, and using vegetable ghee.

Fasulye wah Bandora

[Fas-oo-lee-ya Wah Ban-door-ah]

*Fasulye wah bandora can be served with rice, or as a side with a simple topping of spring onion.
We recommend serving it with Wahiba and Diab's bulgur wheat recipe below.*

Created by Wahiba Al Baratek and Diab Faroukh

 vegan   serves 4   1 hour total time   10 minutes prep time   50 minutes cooking time

METHOD

1. Place a pan over a medium heat and add the oil. When the oil is hot, add the diced onion and stir well. Fry the onion until it softens, then add the green beans and mix well.

2. Add the salt, pepper, chilli powder and turmeric and stir well. Reduce the heat and cover the pan with a lid. Leave the beans to cook for 25 minutes, stirring regularly.

3. Add the chopped tomatoes and stir well before covering the pan with a lid for another 20 minutes, until the sauce is smooth. Add the chopped garlic and cook for a further 5 minutes before taking the mixture off the heat.

INGREDIENTS

½ cup olive oil
1 medium onion, diced
500g green beans
1 tsp salt
½ tsp ground black pepper
½ tsp chilli powder
½ tsp ground turmeric
1 tin of chopped tomatoes
5 cloves of garlic, finely chopped

Bulgur Wheat with Chickpeas

Created by Wahiba Al Baratek and Diab Faroukh

 vegetarian   serves 5   45 hour total time   5 minutes prep time   40 minutes cooking time

METHOD

1. Put a pot over a medium heat and add the oil. When the oil is hot, add the onion along with the salt, turmeric and chilli powder. Stir well and fry the onions until they begin to soften.

2. Add the tinned tomatoes and chickpeas, stir well, then add the water and stir occasionally until the mixture comes to the boil. When the water has started to come to the boil, add the bulgur wheat. Bring the mixture back to the boil then reduce to a low heat and leave the bulgur to cook for 30 minutes until it softens.

3. Stir in the ghee, creating a soft mixture, before serving the dish hot.

INGREDIENTS

¼ cup vegetable oil
1 large onion, diced
1 tbsp salt
¼ tsp ground turmeric
¼ tsp chilli powder
1 tin of chopped tomatoes
2 tins of chickpeas
1 litre water
500g coarse bulgur wheat
1 tbsp ghee

Maklouba

[Mah-kloo-bah]

*Maklouba is a show-stopping meal. Despite how beautiful and detailed it appears,
this meal is cooked frequently by families for any occasion. The different layers include lamb,
rice, chicken and vegetables.*

Created by Malak Al Betare

serves 7 | 3h 30 minutes total time | 2h 30 minutes prep time | 1 hour cooking time

METHOD (for the maklouba)

1. Before you begin, soak the rice in a bowl of water with half a teaspoon of salt for 2 hours.

2. Cut the aubergines in half lengthways and remove the stalks. Sprinkle a little salt over them to prevent them from absorbing too much oil when frying, wiping away any excess water with kitchen roll. Place a pan over a medium heat and add the vegetable oil. When the oil is hot, add the aubergines and fry them until they turn golden brown, no longer than 10 minutes. Leave them to cool.

3. Place a large cooking pot over a medium heat and add the 2 litres of water. When the water has come to the boil, add the chicken. Then add the cinnamon, cardamom, cloves, onion, bay leaves and dried limes. Season the broth with two teaspoons of salt and one teaspoon of black pepper.

4. Stir well, then leave the meat to boil for 45 minutes before removing it from the water. Using a sieve, remove the cinnamon sticks and cloves from the broth. Remove the chicken and save the remaining water for later as it will be used to cook the rice.

5. Place a clean pan over a medium heat and add some ghee. When the ghee has melted, add the meat and fry it for a few minutes until it has browned on both sides. Remove the chicken from the heat and set aside.

6. Add the carrots, tomato and pepper to a large cooking pot. Layer them to cover the base of the pot. Place the fried aubergines on top and season with a pinch of salt and pepper. Follow this by layering the chicken pieces over the aubergine.

7. Wash and drain the soaked rice and place it in the pot over the chicken. Next, pour 6 cups of (or the remaining) hot chicken broth over the rice. Place the pot on the stove on the highest heat and leave it to boil. When it starts to boil taste it to check whether it needs salt or more spice. Add it if so and after that cover the pot with the lid and leave it to cook over the lowest heat until the rice is cooked, approximately 30 minutes. Once cooked, leave the maklouba for about 10 minutes to rest.

TO SERVE

8. Flip the pot with the rice upside down onto a plate so that the vegetables become the top layer of the dish and remove the pan as if revealing a sandcastle! Garnish the maklouba with fried mince lamb and nuts.

INGREDIENTS

for the maklouba:
5 cups basmati rice
5 tsp salt
vegetable oil, for frying
5 large aubergines
2 litres water
1.5kg chicken
2 cinnamon sticks
7 cardamom pods
5 cloves
1 small onion, cut in half
2 bay leaves
2 dried limes
$1\frac{1}{2}$ tsp ground black pepper
ghee, as desired
3 carrots, chopped
2 tomatoes, chopped
1 green or red pepper, chopped

to serve:
350g minced lamb
100g almonds
100g cashews

Kebab Batinjan

The name of this dish means 'kebab with aubergine'. Kebab is a staple food throughout Syria and the Middle East, and like kibbeh, it comes in many forms. Balqis' recipe is closer to the kofte or meatball-style kebab.

Created by Balqis Fakroukh

 serves 6   2 hour total time   30 minutes prep time   1h 30 minutes cooking time

METHOD (for the kebab)

1. Place the lamb and beef into a large mixing bowl. Mix the two together thoroughly. Add the onion, spices and salt then mix thoroughly again, coating the meat evenly. Divide the meat mixture into small, circular, evenly sized patties (about 6-8cm) and leave them to one side.

2. Put a pan on a medium heat before adding the vegetable oil. Remove the stalks from the aubergines and slice them into thin circular sections by cutting across them widthways. Add the sliced aubergine to the hot oil and fry for 15 minutes until it browns, then place the slices on a piece of kitchen roll to absorb any excess oil.

3. Slice the tomatoes and the peppers into circular sections, as with the aubergines. Take a deep ovenproof dish and line the bottom with a meat patty, slice of tomato, slice of fried aubergine then a slice of pepper alternately. Preheat the oven to 180°C.

METHOD (for the sauce)

4. You will need a blender. Put the tomatoes into it and blend them into a smooth sauce. Add the garlic, red pepper and onion along with the salt, black pepper, curry powder and chilli powder or paprika. Blend the sauce until smooth then pour it into a pan. Put the pan over a medium heat until the sauce comes to the boil, then take it off the heat and pour it over the meat and vegetables in the ovenproof dish.

5. Place the dish in the preheated oven for 1 hour 30 minutes.

TO SERVE

6. The dish can be served with Arabic bread or rice. If you choose to serve it with rice, this can be prepared while the main dish is in the oven. Put a pan over a medium heat and add a little olive oil. Cut the vermicelli into 2cm lengths and add it to the hot oil. Stir thoroughly and fry the vermicelli until golden.

7. Add the water and chicken stock to a clean pot. Place the pot over a high heat and add the rice. When the water comes to the boil, reduce the heat and leave the rice to simmer for about 10 minutes, or until it has softened.

8. Place the rice into bowls and top with the fried vermicelli and kebab batinjan.

INGREDIENTS

for the kebab:
500g minced lamb
500g minced beef
1 medium onion
1 tsp black pepper
1 tsp cardamom
1 tsp ground coriander
3 tsp salt
$^1/_2$ cup vegetable oil
3 aubergines
1kg tomatoes
3 peppers (1 red, 1 green, 1 yellow)

for the sauce:
800g tinned tomatoes
5 cloves of garlic, crushed
1 red pepper, chopped
1 medium onion, chopped
1 tsp salt
$^1/_4$ tsp ground black pepper
$^1/_4$ tsp curry powder
1 tsp chilli powder or paprika, as preferred

to serve:
splash of olive oil
500g vermicelli
6 cups water
1 chicken stock cube
3 cups basmati rice,
or Arabic bread if preferred

Mlehy

[M u h - l a y - h e]

Mlehy is a dish made for special occasions, such as weddings. Traditionally, the matriarch of the house would make it for anyone who had been invited to the celebration.

Created by Mona Al Hamadi

serves 5 | 1h 30 minutes total time | 15 minutes prep time | 1h 30 minutes cooking time

METHOD

1. Divide the chickens into their separate parts: legs, wings and breasts. Wash the meat thoroughly before placing the pieces in a large cooking pot. Cover the chicken with fresh water and put the pot over a medium heat. When the water comes to the boil, reduce the heat and place a lid over the pot. Add the onion, one tablespoon of salt and the cardamom. Cover the pot again and leave the broth to cook on a low heat for 45 minutes.

2. When the chicken is cooked, take the pot off the heat. Transfer 16 cups of the water from the chicken pot into a clean pot and place it over a medium heat to come to the boil. Wash and drain the bulgur wheat thoroughly, then add it to the broth. Add a teaspoon of ghee and a pinch of salt then leave the pot over a medium heat until it comes to the boil. At this point, reduce the heat and cover the pot with a lid. Leave it to simmer for 30 minutes, occasionally checking it to remove any foam that may appear on the surface.

3. Pour the yoghurt into a blender. Add the cornflour, flour and egg and mix the ingredients together on a low speed until they are well combined. Pour the mixture into a pan and place it over a medium heat. Stir continuously as this mixture comes to the boil, then reduce to a low heat. Add a pinch of salt and the turmeric then leave the mixture to cook on a low heat for 5 minutes, stirring occasionally. Add the poached chicken to the yoghurt sauce and leave to cook for a further 5 minutes.

4. When the bulgur is cooked, pour it into a large bowl and add the remaining ghee. Mash the bulgur and ghee until the mixture is soft before lining the bottom of a large serving dish with it. Place the chicken on top and cover with the yoghurt sauce to serve.

INGREDIENTS

2 whole chickens
1 small onion, sliced
2 tbsp salt
4 cardamom pods
1kg rough bulgur wheat
2 tsp ghee
2kg plain yoghurt
1 tbsp cornflour
2 tbsp plain flour
1 egg
1 tsp ground turmeric

Fried Fish

This dish puts a Syrian twist on an English favourite. We guarantee that you won't want to eat fried fish any other way once you have tried Diab's recipe.

Created by Wahiba Al Barakat and Diab Faroukh

 serves 6

 2h 30 minutes total time

2 hours soaking time

 15 minutes prep time

 15 minutes cooking time

METHOD

1. Combine the salt, lemon juice, parsley, garlic and spices to make a marinade. Lay the fish fillets into it, massage the marinade into them, cover and leave in the fridge for 2 hours so the fish absorbs the flavours.

2. When the fish has marinated, heat a deep pan half full of vegetable oil. It should be about the right temperature for frying when a piece of bread dropped into the oil sizzles and turns golden. Dredge the fish in the flour so it has a good coating, then carefully lay the fish into the hot oil and fry until golden. Turn the fish occasionally to get an even colour.

INGREDIENTS

2 tbsp salt
4 lemons, juiced
1 bunch of parsley, finely chopped
2 whole bulbs of garlic, finely chopped
1 tsp ground cardamom
1 tsp ground cumin
1 tsp ground turmeric
1 tsp chilli powder
4 whole fish fillets, frozen
1.5 litres vegetable oil
500g plain flour

We serve this fried fish with tahini, yoghurt and lemon and a simple sauce of more chopped parsley, garlic, salt and lemon juice to taste.

Ghraiba

[G r e y - b a]

These little shortbread-like biscuits can be found from Syria all the way to North Africa. In Tunisia, pistachios are replaced by almonds. Either way, ghraiba are a delicious sweet snack.

Created by Edeh Al-Haj-Ali

| vegatarian | serves 8 | 1h 15 minutes total time | 1 hour prep time | 15 minutes cooking time |

METHOD

1. Combine the ghee and icing sugar in a mixing bowl. Stir until they are well combined. When the icing sugar has been absorbed into the ghee, add the flour gradually. Continue stirring the mixture and adding the flour a little at a time until dough forms. Leave the dough in the fridge for 30 minutes.

2. After the dough has been left to cool, take it out of the fridge and place it on a flat surface ready to make the ghraiba. At this point, preheat the oven to 160°C.

3. Take a small section of dough and roll it into a cylinder in your palms. Join the edges of the cylinder together to form a closed doughnut shape and press a pistachio nut into the centre. Repeat until all the dough has been used.

4. Place the ghraiba on a baking tray and put the tray on the bottom shelf of the preheated oven. Leave them to cook for 10 minutes before moving them up to the middle shelf to cook for another 5 minutes. Remove the ghraiba from the oven and leave them to cool for a few minutes before serving.

INGREDIENTS

1 cup ghee
1 cup icing sugar
3 cups plain flour
1 cup whole pistachios

Ma'amoul

[Mah-mool]

Ma'moul is a common sweet that you can find pre-packaged and sold in shops throughout Syria, much like a chocolate bar! But with a recipe as good as Bahea's you will want to try and make this simple sweet at home. Bahea learned this recipe from her mother, Mona.

Created by Bahea Al Nasser

vegan | serves 15-20 | 5h 20 minutes total time | 5 hours prep time | 20 minutes cooking time

METHOD (for the dough)

1. Leave the ghee to reach room temperature. Sift the flour into a large mixing bowl and add the ghee. Gently combine them with your fingers until all of the ghee has been absorbed. Use your hands to form the mixture into a smooth dough. Place the dough in the fridge to cool for 2 hours.

METHOD (for the date filling)

2. Place the mashed dates into a clean bowl and add the two tablespoons of ghee. Mix together well, then divide the mixture into small balls (two balls should fit inside your closed fist) and place them in the fridge to cool.

METHOD (for the sugar syrup)

3. Pour the water into a clean pan, add the sugar and stir continuously until the sugar has dissolved. Put the pan over a medium heat and when the mixture starts to come to the boil, add the lemon juice. Then take the syrup off the heat. Leave to one side.

METHOD (for the ma'amoul)

4. After 2 hours, remove the dough from the fridge. Pour the cold water into a bowl and add the sugar, blossom water and the cooled sugar syrup. Stir well then pour the mixture over the dough. Use your hands to combine the mixture with the dough until it has a soft, sticky texture. Place the dough back in the fridge for 1 hour and 30 minutes.

5. Dust a baking tray with a little flour. Remove the chilled dough from the fridge and separate it into medium-sized balls (twice the size of the date balls). Place them on the baking tray.

6. To form each ma'amoul, press a ball of date filling into a piece of dough and close the dough around it. You can shape the edges with a fork and create a design on top if you so wish. Repeat this step for each piece before placing the tray back in the fridge for 30 minutes. Preheat the oven to 250°C.

7. Place the tray on the middle shelf of the preheated oven and leave the ma'amoul to bake for 15 to 20 minutes, or until they have a golden colour. Remove the tray from the oven and leave the ma'amoul to cool before serving.

INGREDIENTS

for the dough:
1kg plain flour
500g vegetable ghee

for the date filling:
1kg dates, mashed
2 tbsp vegetable ghee, room temperature

for sugar syrup:
1 cup water
2 cups caster sugar
1/2 tsp lemon juice

for the ma'amoul:
1 cup cold water
1 cup granulated sugar
5 tbsp orange blossom water

Barazek

[Bah-re-zek]

Barazek are particularly popular during Eid, along with ma'amoul and ghraiba. This biscuit is used for celebratory events and is often given as a gift at weddings or birthdays.

Created by Asmaa Al Nasser

vegan

serves 15

1h 23 minutes
total time

1h 15 minutes
prep time

8 minutes
cooking time

METHOD

1. Mix the flour and ghee together. Knead the mixture with your hands for about 10 minutes until you get a smooth consistency. Place in the refrigerator for about 15 minutes.

2. Mix the two tablespoons of sugar with the toasted sesame seeds then stir in the three tablespoons of sugar syrup until well mixed. Now add the tablespoon of water and combine until the mixture becomes slightly moist and sticks to the palm of your hand.

3. In a separate bowl, combine the cup of sugar, half cup of water and quarter cup of sugar syrup, then stir well until the sugar has dissolved.

4. Take the dough out of the fridge, then pour the sugar mixture over the cold dough and keep kneading for 10 minutes until the dough no longer sticks to your hands.

5. Dust a clean surface with a little flour and take a small piece of the dough from the ball. Roll it into a long sausage shape, about 2.5cm in diameter. Cut the dough sausage into small pieces, shaping each one into a ball, and put the rest of the dough back in the refrigerator.

6. Place the crushed pistachios on a serving plate. Take one of the dough balls and press it firmly into the nuts until the ball has been flattened into a biscuit shape and the bottom has a good covering.

7. Place the sesame mixture on a separate plate. Flip the biscuit over and press the other side into the sesame mixture, so that the biscuit is coated with pistachios on one side and sesame on the other. Place the biscuit on a tray covered with greaseproof paper. Repeat the same method for the rest of the dough until it has been used up, along with the pistachios and sesame seeds.

8. Preheat the oven to 170°C before baking. Place the tray on the middle shelf of the oven. Remove the barazek after about 8 minutes, or when they turn golden in colour. Remove them from the oven and leave to cool before serving.

INGREDIENTS

500g plain flour, plus extra for dusting
250g vegetable ghee
2 tbsp sugar
500g sesame seeds, toasted
3 tbsp sugar syrup
1 tbsp water
1 cup sugar
$^1/_2$ cup water
$^1/_4$ cup sugar syrup
$^1/_2$ cup crushed pistachios

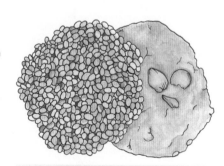

You can also use non-vegetable ghee if you prefer.

Lazakyat

[La-ze-key-at]

If you are tired of the same old lemon and sugar pancakes every Shrove Tuesday, this recipe will add an Arabic twist to your tradition. The walnuts and cashews can be swapped for any nuts of your choice.

Created by Malak Al Betare

 vegetarian   serves 6   35 minutes total time   5 minutes prep time   30 minutes cooking time

METHOD

1. Place the milk, flour and salt in a blender and blend for 3 minutes or until thoroughly combined. Place a frying pan on a high heat. To prevent the pancakes from sticking, put a teaspoon of ghee in the pan. Place one ladle of the batter into the pan, spread the mixture across the whole base, and heat until cooked, exactly like an English pancake. Turn it over and cook the other side, then transfer onto a plate and brush the whole pancake with melted ghee. Sprinkle over one tablespoon of sugar and about a teaspoon each of walnuts and cashew nuts, or more if desired.

2. Repeat this process, layering the pancakes with sugar and nuts as above, until the batter has been used up. To serve, top the pancake stack with coconut shavings and pistachios.

INGREDIENTS

3¹/₂ cups whole milk
2 cups plain flour
pinch of salt
200g ghee, melted
2 cups sugar
150g walnuts, finely chopped
150g unsalted cashew nuts, toasted
100g coconut shavings, for decoration
handful of pistachios, crushed

This can be made vegan by using vegan milk and vegetable ghee.

a family of extraordinary strength

Mona Al Hamadi, Mohammed Al Nasser
and their children, Ismael, Bahea, Asmaa

Written by Rebecca Joy Novell

The Al Nasser family are a family of extraordinary strength. On the surface, they appear as your average, normal, happy family, settled in the heart of Lancashire. Yet, Mona and Mohammed live with the immense struggle of knowing that every day, three of their children remain in horrific conditions in a refugee camp in Jordan. Every day, they battle to be reunited with their children, by speaking to the council, to MPs, to national charities. Yet no progress has been made and there is no hope in sight for a successful reunion. Hours of each day are spent on facetime

to their beloved son and daughters. Every night without her children, is a sleepless night for Mona and the pain it causes Mona, is an obvious cause of immense sadness for her husband.

And yet, despite all of that, every time I visit the Al Nasser family, they welcome me in to their home with generosity like I have never known. And it's not just me; friends from miles around travel to stay with Mona and Mohammed and are invited to treat their house as their own home.

Mona's Fatayer (page 161) was the first breakfast I ever had at her home. When she was out of the room, cooking up our feast in the kitchen, Mohammed took it upon himself to tell me what an enormously strong woman his wife was. He explained how she cared for every aspect of her family's wellbeing and made sure each child was well and happy each day. The respect Mohammed had for Mona shone from his eyes and yet he told me that women are the source of strength, not only for his family but for all Syrian families – and I can't help but believe him.

"we are now separated by geography

Edah Al-Haj-Ali
Written by Edah Al-Haj-Ali

I was born in a small village near Daraa. I grew up with my six brothers and one sister. We were a very close family growing up and still are, although we are now separated by geography. Four of my brothers are now in Jordan and two in Syria. Fortunately, my sister came to England at the same time as me and we now live in the same village in Lancashire.

I left my village when I got married to my husband. My husband was thirty five years older than me and worked in the centre of Daraa as a shopkeeper. We had two beautiful daughters together, Sara and Hajar. I have so many happy memories of Daraa before the war. My husband had a car and so every weekend we would drive to see my family back in the village and spend the nights together eating and enjoying each other's company. My husband also had an olive farm which we would drive to with the girls and spend days working on it together. My husband has sadly passed away now. These memories mean everything to me.

Asmaa Al-Nasser

Written by Rebecca Joy Novell

Asmaa is the youngest daughter of Mona and Mohammed, from Daraa. At 14 years old, she managed to convince us to include her recipe for barazek (page 179) in the book, despite her being too young to come to the food photography studio with us. Somehow, her skills of persuasion resulted in her coming to the studio anyway. Asmaa has inherited all the strength and resilience of her parents. At such a young age she has taken on a lot of grief and pain that most children will fortunately never experience. And yet she grows and laughs and learns, and proves to us that the future of the Syrian people is as bright as ever.

" the future of the Syrian people is as bright as ever

Roman Theatre of Bosra,
District of Daraa, Syria